ROADSIDE PLANTS
of Southern California

Thomas J. Belzer
Professor of Botany
Pasadena City College
Pasadena, California

Photographs by the Author
Illustrations by Kathy Talaro

MOUNTAIN PRESS PUBLISHING COMPANY
MISSOULA 1984

For Marlo, Lori and Brandon

Seventh Printing
January 1998

Library of Congress Cataloging in Publication Data

Belzer, Thomas J.
    Roadside plants of Southern California.

    1. Roadside flora — California, Southern — Identification.   I. Title.
QK149.B44   1984   582.09794'9   83-8082
ISBN 0-87842-158-0

Mountain Press Publishing Company
P.O. Box 2399 • 2016 Strand Avenue
Missoula, Montana 59806

ACKNOWLEDGEMENTS

This publication represents the completion of a project that started in my mind years ago while riding horseback through the mountains of the Pacific Northwest with Dr. Hanly Burton. He pointed out the names of the many wildflowers and trees as we rode along. These experiences provided the early stimulation that I needed to write a book like this one. I will be forever grateful to Dr. Burton for his companionship and eternal patience as I learned the ways of the mountains and its flora over twenty summers.

Marion Patterson, an expert nature photographer, convinced me that taking a quality picture of a plant is no accident. She spent the time with me necessary to learn the basic skills of close-up floral photography while hiking through the Sierras. As I watched her work with a camera I became inspired enough to try it on my own.

Dr. Jack Burk, California State University at Fullerton, taught me a lot about the flora of southern California. We spent many hours together on field trips into the local deserts and mountains where I was able to ask enough questions to slowly learn the flora of this region.

Dr. Richard Shaw, Utah State University, read the manuscript in its early stages and offered some helpful suggestions based on his experiences writing similar books about the plants of Glacier, Yellowstone and Grand Teton National Parks.

Kathy Talaro, a microbiologist, author and artist offered to draw the plants for this project. Her obvious skills with the air-brush have added another dimension to this book. In between drawings she also found time to do some of the early proofreading of the manuscript. A very special thanks to Kathy and to her husband Art who added encouragement along the way.

Finally, I would like to acknowledge the help of Susan Burton who typed the manuscript, to Luz Longa for checking the scientific names, to Kristy Kulberg for completing the final editing and to Harold Benson for his fine example of what an author should be.

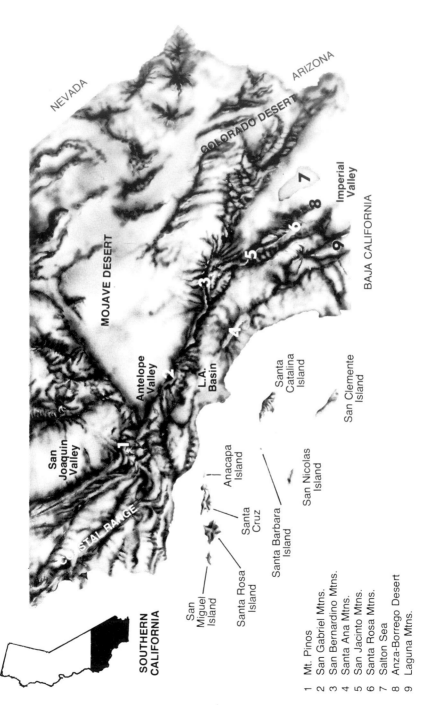

SOUTHERN
CALIFORNIA

NEVADA

ARIZONA

COLORADO DESERT

MOJAVE DESERT

Imperial
Valley

BAJA CALIFORNIA

San Joaquin
Valley

Antelope
Valley

L.A.
Basin

San
Miguel
Island

Santa Rosa
Island

Santa
Cruz
Island

Anacapa
Island

Santa Barbara
Island

San Nicolas
Island

Santa
Catalina
Island

San Clemente
Island

1   Mt. Pinos
2   San Gabriel Mtns.
3   San Bernardino Mtns.
4   Santa Ana Mtns.
5   San Jacinto Mtns.
6   Santa Rosa Mtns.
7   Salton Sea
8   Anza-Borrego Desert
9   Laguna Mtns.

Table of Contents

Date: _____

Family Name _____

Scientific Name _____

Common Name _____

Locality _____

Habitat _____

Remarks _____

Collector _____

4 x 6 Plant Index Card

Introduction

This book is written for the person who enjoys the outdoors and wishes to know more about the native plants of southern California but may not have much botanical training or experience. This photographic field guide is small enough to be taken along on a hike or while traveling on the many roads found throughout southern California. The identification of all native trees in this area, conspicuous shrubs and some of the colorful wildflowers is enhanced through the use of color photography and a leaf index for trees and shrubs. In addition to finding out the name of a native plant, each specimen photographed is described mostly in non-technical terms. Each plant description will include information about its importance, location, family history and economic or cultural value. The plants included in the field guide can be found as one hikes or travels the roadsides through the foothills, mountains, deserts and coastal areas of southern California.

Southern California Climate and Vegetation

All the plants presented in this book can be found in an eight-county area that includes: Santa Barbara, Ventura, Los Angeles, Orange, Riverside, San Diego, Imperial and San Bernardino counties. This is the area that is usually designated as southern California, a region of about 35,000 square miles that is extremely variable in terrain and climate. The elevation ranges from below sea level in some areas of the desert to lofty mountain peaks in excess of 11,000 feet. In the mountains the rainfall may reach 50 inches annually while in the deserts the rainfall is usually less than 10 inches a year. The highest concentration of human population is found in the open valleys, foothills and along the coastal areas. These locations have long been known for their long, dry, warm summers and cool, mild winters. This type of climate has been the largest factor in the development of a vegetation type that is known as the chaparral. This is probably the most widespread plant community in southern California. The plants that dominate this plant community are mostly evergreen shrubs that occur between the deserts and the montane forests. It has been estimated that 70% of this flora has its origins in northern Mexico, having slowly migrated into this area over many millions of years. The ancestry of the rest of the southern California flora is traced to the Sierras, Great Basin Desert and the Rocky Mountains. Many botanists feel that the vegetation in this area is now slowly becoming unique because of its long isolation from the flora of adjacent areas. The Pacific Ocean, high mountain ranges and broad deserts act collectively as significant barriers to the continued migration of plants into and out of southern California.

Diversity of Southern California Habitats

For a number of years there has been a general acceptance of the plant community concept that is used to study broad patterns of vegetation among the California flora. A plant community as originally described by Munz and Keck in 1949 comprises regional vegetation that is characterized by certain dominant plants. Approximately 30 of these plant communities have been described for the state of California. The areas covered by these communities can be very large, i.e., chaparral, or they can be quite small, i.e., salt marshes. Half of these plant communities are found in the southern California area alone. These communities along with a brief description of them are as follows:

Coastal Strand, Coastal Salt Marsh, Freshwater Marsh, Coastal Sage Scrub

These habitats are characterized by dry, rocky slopes and wet lowlands from sea level to about 3000 feet. The annual rainfall is between 10 and 20 inches, and the climate is characterized as moderate due to the proximity of the Pacific Ocean.

Chaparral, Valley Grassland, Southern Oak Woodland

These habitats occur between the previously described plant communities and the montane forests. The dominant plants between 3000 and 5000 feet are the evergreen shrubs and a variety of oak trees. An annual rainfall between 15 and 25 inches produces a dense growth of plants that have gradually become adapted to long, dry, hot summers with frequent fires. The riparian woodland or streamside habitat is found within these communities and is often considered a separate plant community by botanists.

Montane Forest, Bristle-cone Pine Forest

The coniferous forests begin to take over at about 5000 feet and extend into the higher elevations up to 9500 feet. The average rainfall is about 50 inches and the growing season ranges from 3 to 6 months. In southern California the Jeffrey pine and Coulter pine are abundant with the rest of the conifers usually found in smaller populations. The Bristle Cone Forest is found in the mountains adjacent to the Mojave Desert above 8000 feet. This forest will not be included in this field guide. The Bristle-cone pine trees are considered to be the oldest trees found in North America.

Sagebrush Scrub, Shadscale Scrub, Pinyon-Juniper Woodland, Joshua Tree Woodland

These communities are found in the descent from the montane forests inland toward the deserts. Pinyon pines and junipers are seen up to 8000 feet while many of the species of shrubs occur down to 2500 feet. The occurrence of these communities is associated with desert edges on alluvial fans and lower slopes. The average rainfall in these areas ranges from 6 to 20 inches annually.

Creosote Bush Scrub, Alkali Sink

Much of the Colorado and Mojave Desert is covered with scrub vegetation. Creosote Bushes are the dominant shrubs in areas where the soil is not too saline. Alkaline flats in low areas with poor drainage become a common habitat for Saltbushes. The rainfall varies from 2 to 8 inches annually. Temperatures fluctuate widely, and the wind is nearly constant.

Scientific and Common Names of Plants

Most of the native plants of California have two names, a scientific name and a common name. The scientific name is derived from the Latin or Greek language, has information content, and can be recognized by many professional botanists around the world. Common names, on the other hand, are not universally known, are not applied with any set of rules and, consequently, can become quite confusing. Common names do have value, however, since they are often the only names of plants known to a large number of people and may in fact be descriptive, colorful, and even pleasant sounding. The scientific names in use today are based on a simplified form of the binomial system of nomenclature founded by Carolus Linnaeus in 1753. The first part of a scientific name is the genus (plural: genera) and the second part of the name is the specific epithet (the species). In this field guide common names and scientific names will be given for each plant photographed. Additionally, the plant's family will be identified since this information is often useful in identification and in attempting to understand the relationships among the various groups of plants.

Plant Collections and Photography

One of the simplest ways to start a permanent, small collection of plants is to scotch tape a leaf, flower and/or the fruit to a 4 x 6 inch index card (see p. vi). On the opposite side of the card the plant's name, family, habitat and special notes can be recorded. This can be the start of a convenient reference collection that can be used in the future to help identify unknown plants. Index card file boxes can be purchased at most bookstores or stationery stores for the storage of these cards as they begin to accumulate. The colors of the floral structures will eventually begin to fade, but the basic plant characteristics will be left intact for many years. If it is impossible to identify a plant, the specimens could be taken to Rancho Santa Ana Botanic Garden in Claremont, California, where a professional botanist can most likely identify the unknown plant. Over 500,000 plant specimens are maintained in the herbarium at this facility. The Los Angeles County Museum of Natural History has acquired the University of California's native plant collection and now has over 200,000 plant specimens in their herbarium.

It should be noted that it is unlawful to collect plants from many areas. Special permission is needed to collect plants on private property. Special permits are needed to collect plants in national forests. The park superintendent is the only one who can give permission to collect plants in national parks or monuments.

One of the most enjoyable ways to produce a permanent record of a plant found in the field is to take a photograph of it. The new single lens reflex cameras are very easy to operate, and the results are usually very satisfying. It is most convenient to use one of the Macro lenses for close-up photography while in the field. A large variety of other lenses is available for every conceivable application in field photography. For further details consult one of the many good references on field photography that is available in most public libraries. The experience of most field photographers working with plants seems to indicate a preference for Kodachrome 64 film for color slides. This film has a good range of color and speed for photographing most of the native flora. A list of a few of the helpful hints for plant photographers is as follows:

1. Take a lot of time to compose your picture properly. If you rush your work, poor results are more likely.

2. Take many pictures when you find conditions ideal. Shoot both vertical and horizontal positions with different exposures.

3. Become aware of backgrounds. Uncluttered backgrounds usually produce the best pictures. Color highlights in the background can be used to enhance your main subject.

4. It is best to take pictures early in the morning or late in the day. The lighting is usually best at these times.

5. Forget about taking pictures when the wind is blowing. Motion is a major hazard of still photography.

Remember that plants undergo changes during the year corresponding with the change in seasons. It can be rewarding to take a series of photographs of the same plant through its development and year-long life cycle. In southern California field photographers can keep busy with this activity throughout the year working in the desert during the winter months and moving into the mountains as the weather warms up. Many coastal plants bloom during spring and summer months. The photographs of the plants for this book were compiled over a three-year period through changes in seasons and climatic conditions.

How to Use This Book

This field guide is basically organized into five major sections as follows:

1. Ferns and Conifers
2. Broadleaf Trees and Shrubs
3. Vines, Climbers and Parasites
4. Cacti, Sages and Succulents
5. Wildflowers

An unknown plant specimen should first be identified within one of the above five plant sections if possible. After this is done successfully, it is very likely that the unknown plant can be positively identified by comparing it to a color photograph found in this book.

The evergreen and non-flowering plants have been grouped together into the first section. Except for the ferns, none of these plants have very large leaves. The various members of the pine and cypress families fill most of these pages.

Practically all of the native broadleaf trees can be located in the second section. These trees are organized within plant families. This alphabetized listing of common family names includes the common shrubs too. Most of the photographs are close-ups of the leaves and flowers so it will be necessary to look carefully at the plant found in the field when comparing it to one of the photographs.

If the whole plant is vine-like it will likely be found in section three. The parasitic or partially parasitic plants have also been grouped into this part. Parasitic plants found in the field will not be green.

Cacti, sages and succulents are grouped together since many of these plants grow in the same kinds of habitats. These plants seem to be concentrated in the deserts and along the seacoast.

Finally, a few of the more common wildflowers are included in section five. The popular book, *Field Guide to Pacific States' Wildflowers*, has a greater number of wildflowers illustrated and could be used in combination with this reference. The common wildflowers in this section are organized according to color. The color sections are: white flowers, yellow flowers, reddish flowers and blue-purple flowers. Some of the flower colors range in between these pure colors and are grouped with the flowers they approximately match.

xi

Botanical Resources
of Southern California

Southern California has a good variety of habitats for native plants: mountains, deserts, foothills and seashore. These regions are within reach of almost everyone who drives a car, and southern Californians have the reputation for being a very mobile group. Plants found within this field guide are usually not found along freeways but rather along back roads away from cities. A map from the Automobile Association of Southern California or another source will reveal hundreds of miles of roads through most of the plant communities in this area. Some of the more popular highway routes are the Palms To Pines Highway from Palm Desert to Idyllwild; the Angeles Crest Highway and the Ortega Highway. There are many other scenic highways that can be traveled by bicycle, motorcycle or automobile to study the native flora.

An ideal way to study and enjoy plants is to take a hike through one of the national forests. The San Gabriel, San Bernardino and Cleveland National Forests have many well-maintained trails through the foothills and into the high country. John W. Robinson's book, *Trails of the Angeles* describes 100 hikes through the San Gabriel Mountains. One of the most popular hikes is to the top of Mt. Baden-Powell from Vincent Gap. It is this hike that reveals the ancient Limber Pines, a large population of Lodgepole Pines and magnificent views of the Mojave Desert. Other spectacular hikes are to San Gorgonio Peak, elevation 11,485 feet and to San Jacinto Peak, elevation 10,805 feet.The Palm Springs Tram can be taken part way up to San Jacinto Peak leaving only a day's hike to the top and back down again. These hikes and many more can be taken to see the plants included in this field guide.

For the non-hiker, southern California flora can be studied in a less demanding way that will still allow one to be outdoors. Nature centers and parks in all the counties throughout southern California have many native plants and information about them on the grounds. There are usually trained naturalists available to lead small groups through these centers when a reservation is made ahead of time. Finally, this area also has about a dozen botanical gardens and arboreta open without charge to the public. The Botanical Gardens at Santa Barbara and at Claremont are excellent places for studying and enjoying a great variety of native California plants. A partial listing of these nature centers, parks and botanical gardens is as follows:

NATURE CENTERS AND PARKS: LOS ANGELES COUNTY

Antelope Valley Poppy Reserve, 15101 W. Lancaster Rd., Lancaster, California 93534.

Devil's Punchbowl Regional Park, 2800 Devil's Punchbowl Road, Pearlblossom, California 93563.

Eaton Canyon Nature Center, 1750 North Altadena Drive, Pasadena, California 91107.

Earthside Nature Center, 3160 E. Del Mar Blvd., Pasadena, California 91107.

Placerita Canyon Park and Nature Center, 19151 Placerita Canyon Road, Newhall, California 91321.

Topanga Canyon State Park, Malibu Mountains, 20825 Entrada Road, Topanga, California 90290.

Griffith Park, 5375 Red Oak Drive, Los Angeles, California 90028.

NATURE CENTERS AND PARKS: ORANGE COUNTY

Caspers Regional Park at Starr-Viejo Ranch, 33401 Ortega Highway, P. O. Box 395, San Juan Capistrano, California 92675.

Irvine Park, 21401 Chapman Avenue, Orange, California 92669.

Oak Canyon Nature Center, 6700 Walnut Canyon Road, Anaheim, California 92807.

NATURE CENTERS AND PARKS: RIVERSIDE COUNTY

Living Desert Reserve, 47-900 Portola Road, Palm Desert, California 92260.

Mount San Jacinto State Park, P. O. Box 308, Idyllwild, California 92349.

NATURE CENTERS AND PARKS: SAN BERNARDINO COUNTY

Desert Interpretive Center, 831 Barstow Road, Barstow, California 92311.

Joshua Tree National Monument

Twentynine Palms Oasis Visitor Center, Joshua Tree National Monument, 74485 Palm Vista, Twentynine Palms, California 92277.

NATURE CENTERS AND PARKS: SAN DIEGO AND IMPERIAL COUNTIES

Anza Borrego State Park, Borrego Springs, California 92004.

Cuyamaca Ranch State Park, Cuyamaca Star Route, Julian, California 92036.

Palomar Mountain State Park, Palomar Mountain, California 92060.

Torrey Pines State Reserve, Del Mar, California 92077.

BOTANICAL GARDENS

Descanso Gardens, 1418 Descanso Drive, La Canada, California 91011.

Rancho Santa Ana Botanic Garden, 1500 North College Avenue, Claremont, California 91711.

University of California at Riverside Botanic Gardens, University of California, Riverside, California 92502.

Santa Barbara Botanic Garden, Inc., 1212 Mission Canyon Road, Santa Barbara, California 93105.

Los Angeles State and County Arboretum, 301 North Baldwin Avenue, Arcadia, California 91006.

University of California at Los Angeles Botanical Garden-Herbarium Botany Building, Room 124, Los Angeles, California 90024.

Sherman Foundation Center, 2647 East Pacific Coast Highway, Corona Del Mar, California 92625.

Moorten Botanic Garden and Cactarium, 1702 South Palm Canyon Drive, Palm Springs, California 92262.

Huntington Library and Botanical Gardens, 1151 Oxford Road, San Marino, California 91108.

South Coast Botanic Garden, 26701 Rolling Hills Rd., Palos Verdes Peninsula, California 90274.

PONDEROSA PINE

MAIDENHAIR FERN

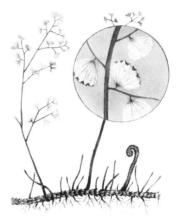

CALIFORNIA JUNIPER

WHITE FIR

Ferns & Conifers

Scientists who have studied the origin of life generally agree that the first living cells originated in the ancient seas well over three billion years ago. From these first cells evolved simple aquatic plants called algae (seaweeds), which, in turn, eventually gave rise to the various land plants. The first land plants to appear were ferns and mosses. Both of these need an aquatic environment to successfully complete their reproductive cycles, so they have not become adapted to a life completely out of water. These spore-producing plants and others like them (horsetails and tree ferns) formed extensive forests during the carboniferous geological period. The descendants of these first landplants were the gymnosperms, more popularly known as conifers. The conifers developed special reproductive structures called cones. The leaves of the conifers became modified into a variety of shapes: needle-like, linear and scaly. The types of cones and the shapes of the leaves are two important characteristics used in classifying conifers. Conifers are subdivided into the cypress and pine families.

Horsetail

Equisetum spp.

These spore-producing plants are found in all parts of the world except Australia. Their unbranched stems have deposits of silicon dioxide which add strength and protect the stem from insects, but which are also known to be poisonous to livestock. The stems have cone-like, spore-producing structures at the ends of the branches. The common horsetail, *E. arvense,* grows in moist locations below 10,000 feet throughout most of the United States.

Polypody

Polypodium californicum

The Polypody fern family is a very large family of over 150 genera and probably more than 7,000 species world-wide. This genus is widely distributed in mostly tropical and semitropical areas. The California Polypody has a creeping rhizome and the distinctive fronds are not evergreen. The sori are round, rather large and each born at the end of a free veinlet. The name Polypody is from the Greek polys (many) and pous (foot) referring to the numerous knob-like protuberances on the rhizome. This fern is found below 4000 feet along moist banks or rock ledges. The bracken fern, which is very common in southern California, looks similar to the Polypody except it has a nearly continuous band of sporangia at the margin of the leaf segment.

Joint Fir

Ephedra spp.

This primitive plant is also known as Mormon tea and Mexican tea. It is a single genus with worldwide distribution although it tends to be concentrated in the southwestern United States. The stems are usually yellow-green, jointed and grooved. The leaves are scale-like with small, dense cone clusters. Joint firs are seen growing on dry slopes, fans and washes along the deserts. Some of the species provide winter forage for grazing animals. A mild tea serving as a tonic can be made from the dried stems. The tonic is used to cure a variety of illnesses. The drug, ephedrine, is extracted from an Asiatic species.

Incense Cedar

Calocedrus decurrens

This handsome evergreen tree grows to about 35 meters among other conifers in forests between 4500 and 8200 feet. This is the only true cedar native to southern California. It is often mistaken for a redwood tree. The bark of the incense cedar is cinnamon-brown, the leaves are scale-like but very flattened and the cones are quite small — about the size of an almond. The cones produce only two edible seeds. The pollen of this tree is produced during the winter months and is a cause of hay fever. After the first few years of growth, it begins to grow moderately fast, thus having some value as an ornamental tree. The wood has been used for shingles, fencing, railroad ties and similar products for construction.

Horsetail

Joint Fir

Polypody

Incense Cedar

Cypress

Cupressus forbesii

Tecate cypress and Cuyamaca cypress, *C. stephensonii,* are the only two species of cypress native to southern California. Tecate cypress is found in the Santa Ana Mountains and in a few localities in San Diego County. This cypress prefers to grow on north slopes where there is some moisture at an elevation between 1500 and 5000 feet. Tecate cypress grows to about ten meters tall. Cuyamaca cypress has a more limited range, growing only on the southwestern slopes of Cuyamaca Peak in San Diego County. Here this rare plants occurs as a shrub; larger specimens apparently have been destroyed by fire. The bark of both species is exfoliating, mahogany-brown, and the leaves are gray-green and scale-like. The walnut-sized cones may not open up for several years.

California Juniper

Juniperus californica

This evergreen shrub is the most common southern California juniper. It is found below 5000 feet in chaparral, pinyon-juniper woodland and other inland plant communities. This plant is usually found as a large shrub. The leaves are scale-like, closely appressed and pointed. The berries are bluish at first but turn reddish-brown as they mature. These berries have been used by California Indians to make a ground meal. The leaves can be used to make a soothing tea. Junipers prefer sun but will grow in the shade of other trees. Their ornamental value is seen in their drought-resistant qualities and tolerance for many soil types.

Western Juniper

Juniperus occidentalis

This juniper is also known as sierra juniper. It is more common in the Sierra Nevada Mountains than in the southern California mountains. This is the largest of the junipers, growing to twenty meters tall and having a well-defined trunk with reddish-brown bark. Junipers are known to live a very long time. One specimen of western juniper of the San Gabriel Mountains in Ice House Canyon stands over thirty meters tall and is estimated to be over 3000 years old. Most of the larger trees in the San Bernardino and San Gabriel Mountains are found growing along ridges in isolation between 6900 and 7900 feet.

Utah Juniper

Juniperus osteosperma

The Utah juniper has a limited range in southern California. This arborescent shrub is fund growing in between California juniper and western juniper on desert slopes of the San Bernardino Mountains between 4800 and 8500 feet. The center of this juniper's distribution is in Utah with shrub forms extending north into Wyoming and southern Idaho. Many tree forms are found near Bridgeport, California in Mono county.

Cypress

California Juniper

Western Juniper

Utah Juniper

Jeffrey Pine

Pine Family
(Pinaceae)

Pinus jeffreyi

This well known conifer is almost exclusively a California tree although a few grow as far north as Oregon. In this area Jeffrey pine is far more common than ponderosa pine. Since these two trees hybridize, it is often difficult to separate the two species. Jeffrey pine grows between 6000 and 8000 feet in serpentine soils forming dense stands in some areas. This three-needled pine has dark, often chocolate-brown bark that smells like vanilla. The cones are pineapple-shaped and smooth to the touch. The wood has been used in construction for years. An important chemical, abietin, is isolated from Jeffrey pine.

Ponderosa Pine

Pine Family
(Pinaceae)

Pinus ponderosa

Ponderosa pine has a wide distribution throughout the Pacific Northwest that rivals lodgepole pine. Ponderosa pine does not range into the northern areas as far as lodgepole pine, however. Ponderosa grows slightly taller than Jeffrey, up to seventy meters. This tree's preferred habitat is gently rolling or flat terrain. These trees grow extremely large on level terrain creating a park-like appearance in isolated areas, such as the Bob Marshall Wilderness in Montana. Ponderosa pine's bark is yellow and plate-like. The cones are smaller than the Jeffrey pines' and prickly to the touch. Smog is killing many of these trees in southern California. As a timber tree ponderosa pine ranks third, exceeded only by Douglas fir and southern yellow pine.

Digger Pine

Pine Family
(Pinaceae)

Pinus sabiniana

Digger pine, also known as gray pine and bull pine, is found mostly in northern California, but a few trees are found in Santa Barbara and Los Angeles counties. Digger pines are concentrated below 4500 feet along the central valley of California. This three-needled pine is easily recognizable in the field by its gray-green foliage, which gives the tree a ghost-like appearance from a distance. This tree also has a habit of growing at right angles to the slope. Digger wood is of poor quality, the seeds are edible, and the tree only lives to be about seventy years old.

Coulter Pine

Pine Family
(Pinaceae)

Pinus coulteri

This common southern California conifer is found growing between 4000 and 7000 feet but rarely in pure stands. Coulter pine has very long needles — the longest of the three-needled pines — and extremely large cones with edible seeds. Coulter pines reach their best development in the San Bernardino Mountains at 5000 feet between the chaparral and Jeffrey pines. The wood is soft, coarse-grained and of poor quality. It is never a good idea to pitch a tent or position a sleeping bag directly under these trees because the cones can drop off at any time and cause injury.

Jeffrey Pine

Digger Pine

Ponderosa Pine

Coulter Pine

Sugar Pine

Pine Family
(Pinaceae)

Pinus lambertiana

Sugar pine is a stately, five-needled pine with short needles and very long cones. From a distance the long, sweeping branches can be seen drooping from the weight of cones clustered at the ends of the branches. Sugar pines are the tallest of the eighty species of pines occurring in the northern hemisphere, growing up to seventy-five meters in the Cascades, Sierras, Coast Ranges and Baja California. This tree is known to live for 500 years. In southern California sugar pines were once more numerous, and in certain areas dominated the forest. The wood from this tree is soft, light and so used in construction that many forests have been severely reduced by logging. These trees grow above 6500 feet.

Limber Pine

Pine Family
(Pinaceae)

Pinus flexilis

Limber pine is another five-needled pine that grows at higher elevations in southern California beginning at 8500 feet. Some of the trees live to 1000 years, second only to the bristlecone pines in longevity. Limber pines are reported growing as far north as Alberta, Canada. The bark of this tree is grayish, and the branches are so flexible at the ends that they can be tied in knots. The cones are very pitchy. On Mt. Baden-Powell many limber pines grow magnificently along ridges and dry slopes facing out into the Mojave Desert below.

Lodgepole Pine

Pine Family
(Pinaceae)

Pinus murrayana

Also known as tamarac pine, lodgepole pine ranges from southern California to Alaska. This species may or may not be distinct from *P. contorta,* found along the northern coast and the Rockies. Lodgepole pine covers over a million square miles throughout the Pacific Northwest and is listed as the seventh most common pine tree in North America. At lower elevations it can succeed itself after a fire and tends to grow in dense thickets. In southern California it is found most commonly at higher elevations where it becomes a large, stately tree. The bark is light-brown and scaly. The needles are short and in bundles of two. The cones are small and walnut-size with a tendency to persist on the trees for years. Although uncommon in southern California, an excellent stand is seen along the north slopes of Mt. Baden-Powell at 7500 feet.

Pinyon Pine

Pine Family
(Pinaceae)

Pinus monophylla

Also known as nut pines, pinyon pines grow at lower elevations along the desert slopes in southern California. *P. monophylla,* the most common species, is a single-needled tree while *P. edulis* and *P. quadifolia* have two and four needles respectively. The seeds are edible. These trees associate with junipers growing as far north as Idaho and south into Baja California.

Sugar Pine

Limber Pine

Lodgepole Pine

Pinyon Pine

Big-cone Douglas Fir

Pine Family
(Pinaceae)

Pseudotsuga macrocarpa

Big-cone Douglas fir, also known as big-cone spruce, is a close relative of well known Douglas fir, *P. menziesii,* a tree that has been logged for years in the Pacific Northwest. Big-cone Douglas fir by comparison has an inferior wood and is not used in construction. The needle-like leaves are arranged spirally around the stems. The cones are twice as large as those of the Douglas fir and characterized by thick scales and small bracts. The long, sweeping branches impart a similarity in appearance to sugar pines. This tree grows at lower elevations, however, beginning at 2000 feet and sometimes extending into the montane forest at 6000 feet.

White Fir

Pine Family
(Pinaceae)

Abies concolor

This is the most widely distributed fir tree in the United States. This is the only true fir found in southern California. It grows on moist slopes between 4500 and 8200 feet. White firs are conspicuous in the forest because of their large size (fifty meters), gray bark and bluish-green needles. The older needles are flattened and erect on the stems. The cones are pitchy and found on older trees near the top in an erect position. A few pure stands of white fir are found on the northern and eastern slopes of the San Gabriel and San Bernardino Mountains. The true firs, also known as balsams, are the source of pitch used to produce lacquer and cementing materials.

Torrey Pine

Pine Family
(Pinaceae)

Pinus torreyana

This conifer is definitely a rare tree found only along the coast near Del Mar in San Diego County and at the eastern end of Santa Rosa Island, one of the eight Channel Islands near the southern California coast. This five-needled pine grows very slowly and does not live much beyond 100 years. Torrey pines grow in a sprawling pattern to about seven meters. The cones are nearly the same size as digger pine cones. The seeds of these cones are very attractive to insects, birds and rodents which is true of most conifers. When Torrey pines are grown as ornamentals, the trees grow much taller than in their native habitat.

Knobcone Pine

Pine Family
(Pinaceae)

Pinus attenuata

Although not very common in southern California, knobcone pine has its main local population centers in the Santa Ana and San Bernardino Mountains. This three-needled pine with many fist-sized cones attached directly to the main branches is usually seen growing below 4000 feet. The cones remain closed and open only after fire. The seeds germinate rapidly after dropping to the ground and produce a thick knobcone forest in areas that have been burned. These trees rarely grow beyond twelve meters tall. It is common to find them planted along highways.

Big-Cone Douglas Fir

White Fir

Torrey Pine

Knobcone Pine

VALLEY OAK

CHAMISE

CALIFORNIA-BAY

MANZANITA

Broadleaf Trees and Shrubs

All modern botanists trace flowering plants to a possible ancestry among seed ferns. It is very likely that the earliest flowering plants were shrubs rather than trees. There is a great variety of shrubs in southern California. The most extensive development of these plants is seen in the plant community in the foothills known as the chaparral. Shrubs are recognized by their tough, woody multi-stems with a small trunk diameter. The typical shrub growing in southern California is hard-leaved, usually evergreen and often spiny.

Trees are described by most botanists as having a strong main trunk covered with bark. Trees reach their greatest development in regions where the climate is mild and there is an abundance of moisture. The generally arid climate of southern California is a factor that has limited the number of different tree species to about fifty natives. The photographs will show the variation in size, shape and appearance among these native trees.

Barberry

Barberry Family
(Berberidaceae)

Berberis amplectens

Barberries are members of a rather widely distributed family of plants in the northern hemisphere. *B. amplectens* is common in the forests and chaparral areas of Riverside and San Diego counties. Nevin's barberry, *B. nevinii*, is a native plant found in the San Fernando valley and is rarely seen growing in the wild. Nevin's barberry has been cultivated for many years and is seen as an ornamental with much potential since it is resistant to drought. The ornamental use of barberries usually involves planting several shrubs into a hedge. The holly-like green leaves and bluish berries make it an attractive plant. The leaves of several barberry species will turn reddish in the shade. The roots and bark have been used by California Indians as a source of dye for their cloth. Wheat rust, a serious fungal plant disease affecting wheat, uses barberry, *B. vulgaris,* as an intermediate host during its life cycle.

Buckeye

Buckeye Family
(Hippocastanaceae)

Aesculus californica

Also commonly known as horse-chestnut, this is the only southern California member of the buckeye family, a small group of trees and shrubs. The only reported location of this shrub is on the dry slopes and canyons of northern Los Angeles County. Large buckeye shrubs grow up to ten meters tall in a spreading type of growth. The leaves are palmately compound, deciduous and folded down the length of the midrib. The flowers appear in late May as clusters of white blossoms. A large, single seed which is pear-shaped and poisonous is produced by late fall. California Indians were known to grind up these seeds and sprinkle them into ponds to stupefy the fish. In the winter months this shrub has an almost ghost-like appearance because of its gray-white, smooth bark.

Wild Buckwheat

Buckwheat Family
(Polygonaceae)

Eriogonum fasciculatum

Wild buckwheat is the most common southern California member of this large family of shrubs and herbs. Family members that are best known are the cultivated buckwheat and rhubarb. Members are recognized in the field by their compact flowers and their reputation for the production of sour juice. Wild buckwheat occurs along the roads of southern California and in other areas below 3000 feet. The leaves are small, linear, leathery and evergreen. The flowers are white or rose-pink. The dried flowers persist on the shrubs long after the blooming period. Several species of *Eriogonum,* an extremely large genus, occur in the high mountains in habitats that are harsh. An examination of the flower usually is enough to identify these plants. Buckwheat flour is made from the related species, *Pagopyrum spp.,* which is not found in California.

Barberry

Buckeye

Buckeye

Wild Buckwheat

Desert Willow

Bignonia Family
(Bignoniaceae)

Chilopsis linearis

Desert willow, also known as desert catalpa, is a large desert shrub or tree that is the only member of this family found in southern California. Several members of this family centered in the tropics are cultivated for their showy flowers. This plant grows up to five meters tall in both the Mojave and Colorado deserts. Desert willow is usually mistaken for a willow because of its willow-like leaves, spreading branches and crooked trunk. The violet-scented, orchid-like flowers appear in April and can still be found into July. A tea can be made from the dried flowers or seed pods. When used as an ornamental, a loose, sandy soil is required because of this shrub's preference for growing in desert washes.

White Alder

Birch Family
(Betulaceae)

Alnus rhombifolia

This tall tree is a member of a small family of deciduous trees and shrubs found mostly in the temperate areas of the northern hemisphere. White alder and water birch, *Betula fontinalis,* are the only species found in this area. Water birch is not common, being reported growing only in the Panamint and White Mountains. This is the only birch found here from about forty species in the northern hemisphere. White alders usually grow along water courses with the cottonwoods and willows. This tree is easily recognized by its gray-white bark and egg-shaped, toothed, yellow-green, simple leaves. The male and female flowers form catkins, which are a source of allergies for some people. The fruit, when produced, is an unusual cone-like structure called a strobile. This tree does not have the economic value of red alder, *Alnus rubra.* Red alder is found along the northern California coast and is the leading hardwood in the Pacific Northwest. This tree is used for pulpwood, making furniture, and as a fuel.

Jojoba

Box Family
(Buxaceae)

Simmondsia chinensis

Jojoba, also called the goatnut, is a member of a small family of trees, shrubs and herbs. This is the only representative from this family found in California. Jojoba is a shrub that is known for its long life (100 years) and preference for growing on dry, rocky hillsides below 5000 feet. The shrub grows to about two meters high and has stiff branches and leathery, oblong-ovate leaves. The flowers are small, greenish and seen from March through May. The fruit is a nut-like capsule with a large oily seed. The seed is edible and the source of a rich drink. Jojoba oil is an excellent substitute for sperm whale oil, a discovery which has renewed interest in cultivating this shrub for commercial purposes. The oil is used in the preparation of hair tonics, shampoos, and some pharmaceuticals. Chemically the oil is a liquid wax that is hydrogenated into a colorless material like beeswax. Large scale cultivation is planned for this shrub.

Desert Willow

White Alder

Water Birch

Jojoba

Coffeeberry

Buckthorn Family
(Rhamnaceae)

Rhamnus californica

Coffeeberry is a large shrub with a wide range of distribution growing on slopes from 3500 to 7000 feet. Some species of coffeeberry are reported to have medicinal value. The berries of this species have no caffeine in them. The leaves are oblong and found throughout the year. The inconspicuous flowers develop into berries that change from red to black as they mature. The related species, *R. purshiana*, called cascara sagrada has been used by California Indians as a laxative and a tonic for centuries. The outer bark of both species can be used as a laxative. These shrubs can best be identified in the field by their dark green leaves, berries and relatively large size. The southern California species, *R. californica*, grows up to four meters tall in moist habitats.

Redberry

Buckthorn Family
(Rhamnaceae)

Rhamnus crocea

This is a low-growing evergreen shrub that grows only one meter or less in height. Redberry is usually found growing in dry washes and canyons below 3000 feet. The branches of this shrub are very rigid and spinose. The flowers are small and inconspicuous, but the berries are bright red, which brings attention to this shrub during summer and fall. Holly-leaved coffeeberry, *R. ilicifolia*, is a larger shrub found in the San Jacinto and Santa Ana Mountains on slopes below 5000 feet. This shrub flowers from February through April and produces bright red berries by mid-summer. Some of the leaves are "notched," which is a field characteristic often used to distinguish this shrub from holly-leaved cherry, *Prunus ilicifolia*.

Ceanothus

Buckthorn Family
(Rhamnaceae)

Ceanothus spp.

Also referred to as the California lilac, *ceanothus* is very well represented in southern California with at least seventeen species found here. Many of these species hybridize freely so the individual species are difficult to separate. Palmer's ceanothus, *C. palmeri*, is a large spreading shrub with gray-green bark and long, flexible branches. The leaves are persistent, light green and somewhat leathery. The showy flower clusters are first seen in May and later into June. Palmer's ceanothus is found growing on dry slopes between 3200 and 6000 feet in the mountains of Los Angeles, Orange and San Diego counties. It is estimated that there are at least sixty species of ceanothus, all native to North America. Several species are used ornamentally.

Coffeeberry

Holly-leaved Redberry/Coffeeberry

Ceanothus

Desert Ceanothus

Buckthorn Family
(Rhamnaceae)

Ceanothus greggii

As its name implies, this shrub is commonly found near the deserts on slopes between 3500 and 7000 feet. This shrub never grows more than two meters tall. The branches are rigid with numerous, small, gray-green leaves that are commonly concave above. The flowers are cream-white found in umbrella-like clusters in May and June. The fruit is a capsule. It is common to find this shrub associated with pinyon pines and california junipers.

Hairy Ceanothus

Buckthorn Family
(Rhamnaceae)

Ceanothus oliganthus

This large, spineless shrub is found below 4500 feet in the foothills of southern California. It is often found growing in the same locality as hoary-leaf ceanothus, *C. crassifolius*. Hoary-leaf ceanothus has white flowers, white pubescense and brown stipules. Hairy ceanothus has ovate, evergreen leaves with three main veins and small hairs on both sides of the leaves. The flowers are deep blue or purple, fading to almost white as they mature. Both species are particularly common on the south slopes of the San Gabriel Mountains.

Deerbrush

Buckthorn Family
(Rhamnaceae)

Ceanothus integerrimus

Deerbrush is a large, bright green, deciduous, delicately branched shrub that appears to be somewhat drooping. This shrub has no spines, feels soft, and has green bark. The leaves have one main vein and are pale green. The flower clusters are whitish. This ceanothus is commonly found in the mountains of the Sierras and in southern California between 3500 and 7500 feet. The common name, deerbrush, is given because this shrub is a favorite browse of deer. This species is usually found in moist locations. All plants will stump-sprout after cutting.

Chaparral Whitethorn

Buckthorn Family
(Rhamnaceae)

Ceanothus leucodermis

Chaparral whitethorn is a tall, stout shrub with spinose branches which are usually gray-white in color. The leaves are oblong-ovate with three main veins originating from the base. The flower clusters are simple, short and vary from bluish to white. The flowers appear from April to June. This shrub is a common member of the chaparral plant community growing below 6000 feet on dry, rocky slopes. This species has been used with some success in southern California to control soil erosion on hillsides.

Desert Ceanothus
Deerbrush

Hairy Ceanothus
Chaparral Whitehorn

Flannel Bush

Fremontodendron californicum

Flannel bush belongs to a family of trees, shrubs and herbs that are centered mostly in the tropics. Chocolate comes from the fermented seeds of one species within this family, and the presence of fine hairs over much of the herbage is characteristic of the plants. The leaves of flannel bush are fig-like, flannel-feeling, alternate and usually three-lobed. This shrub can attain heights up to 3.5 meters when growing in gravelly washes. The flowers are a brilliant lemon-yellow usually appearing in late May. General John C. Fremont discovered this plant in 1846 during an expedition through the Sierras. A significant population occurs east of Wrightwood growing on steep slopes and in a dry river bed.

In San Diego County, *F. Mexicana* is found growing in isolated locations in dry canyons below 1500 feet. This species is particularly tolerant to drought and sea-coast conditions. Both species have been used ornamentally in Europe and in this country for years. The Indians are reported to have made a crude type of rope from the tough bark of these plants. The common name, Leatherwood, is used in reference to this rope-making practice.

Bladderpod

Isomeris arborea

Bladderpod, also referred to as burro fat, is the most common member of this tropical family found in southern California. This is the only shrub-member found in this area. Many of the species within this plant group are xerophytes with limited use as ornamentals. The leaves of bladderpods are gray-green, alternate, trifoliate and only slightly petioled. The bright yellow flowers and excerted stamens are seen most times of the year. The fruit is very distinctive consisting of inflated capsules that are equally divided. The herbage is extremely foul-smelling, a trait that explains the label "skunk among plants" often given it. Bladderpod has a wide distribution growing on the hills, bluffs and stabilized dunes of the sea coast and ranging into the desert edges. Recent research indicates that this shrub is relatively non-flammable and will not support an open flame when ignited. It has consequently been considered for replanting burned hillsides in southern California where fire is a constant problem near residences. The salad seasoning "capers" comes from some species within this family. Bladderpod fruit is reported to taste like radish.

Flannel Bush

Flannel Bush

Bladderpod

Creosote Bush

Caltrop Family
(Zygophyllaceae)

Larrea tridentata

This erect, diffusely branched evergreen shrub is a member of the Caltrop family which is centered in Australia and South Africa. The most common species within this family found in the arid regions of North America is creosote bush. In many areas of the desert it is the only noticeable vegetation. When the soil becomes too salty for the creosote, another genus, *Atriplex spp.,* saltbush dominates. The leaves of creosote bush are small, dark green and leathery. The stems are dark brown or almost black. Yellow flowers that appear in spring mature into fuzzy seed-balls by early summer. The resinous quality of the stems gives this shrub many medicinal uses. Dr. Vasek, U C Riverside, has recently found an 11,700-year-old ring of creosote bushes in the Mojave Desert.

Dogwood

Dogwood Family
(Cornaceae)

Cornus occidentalis

Dogwoods are tall, spreading shrubs found in moist habitats below 8000 feet. Most dogwoods are found along streams in shaded spots. This genus is the only representative of the family found in the United States. The leaves of *C. occidentalis* are broad, slightly paler beneath and turn reddish-brown in the fall months. The flowers are found in umbrella-like clusters, whitish and flat-topped. The generic name *Cornus* (horn) is in reference to the very hard wood of the dogwoods. Western dogwoods are more common in the Sierras and Cascades. Several species cultivated as ornamentals are particularly well developed in the southeastern region of the United States.

Hackberry

Elm Family
(Ulmaceae)

Celtis reticulata

Hackberry is an uncommon tree and the only native member of this family found in southern California. Hackberry is a small, spreading tree found in a few places between 2800 and 5000 feet in the Laguna Mountains and in an isolated stand near Banning, California. Plants within this family are known to have watery juice and alternate, simple, deciduous leaves with stipules. The fruit is a samara, nut or drupe. The well known elm, *Ulmus spp.,* has become a naturalized tree in many areas of California. Several species are used ornamentally, and some are considered as weed trees,

Snapdragon Penstemon

Figwort Family
(Scrophulariaceae)

Keckiella antirrhinoides

Snapdragon penstemon is a shrub obviously in close relationship with the herbaceous penstemons. This shrub grows best on north-facing slopes below 4000 feet. A relatively new genus, *Keckiella,* is represented by five species, all found in southern California. Its leaves are linear, entire, and very crowded on the much-branched stems. The flowers are bright yelow in the spring and look like the well known cultivated snapdragon flowers. Many of these shrubs can be seen on the north-facing slopes of Mt. San Jacinto.

Creosote Bush

Dogwood

Hackberry

Snapdragon Penstemon

Western Azalea

Rhododendron occidentale

Western Azalea is a handsome, loosely branched shrub with deciduous leaves and stiff twigs. The leaf blades are elliptic, simple and slightly hairy. The large, white flowers occur in clusters at the ends of the branches in May through July and are very fragrant and showy. This species is found growing as far north as southern Oregon. Western azalea grows in semi-shaded locations usually along water courses between 4500 and 7300 feet in southern California. The San Jacinto Mountains and the Cuyamaca Mountains are its only reported locations. The California rosebay, R. macrophyllum, is the species usually cultivated, and although it grows naturally as far north as Canada, it is not native to southern California.

Elderberry

Sambucus mexicana

Mexican elderberry is easily the most common species of elderberry found in this area. The honeysuckle family consists of small trees, shrubs or vines. Mexican elderberry is a small tree found in open flats and valleys below 4500 feet. The leaves are opposite, pinnately compound with from five to nine leaflets. The pithy branches form the basis for this species' name. Sambucus refers to the musical instrument called the sambuke that is made from the soft wood of this species. The creamy-white flowers arranged in umbrella-like clusters appear in late spring. The berries may be either blue or white and can be eaten only after they are fully ripe. Blue elderberry, S. caerula, is a less common species found at higher elevations within the montane forest. Blue elderberry is found as far north as British Columbia. Red elderberry, S. microbotrys, is a species of elderberry found growing in the Sierras. Its red berries and dark green foliage make it a very striking shrub.

Snowberry

Symphoricarpus spp.

It is represented by three species in southern California. Symphoricarpus means clusters of fruits. These shrubs have small clusters of white, ovoid, two-seeded berries. The snowberries are small and delicately branched. The leaves are simple with fine hairs which makes them feel very soft. Flowers bloom from April to June and are bell-shaped, pink or white, and ill-smelling. S. mollis is the species found within the chaparral plant community below 5000 feet. The berries are edible and serve as food for many animals. The young stems are crushed for an extract that is used to cure certain stomach disorders.

Western Azalea

Elderberry

Snowberry

Manzanita

Heath Family
(Ericaceae)

Arctostaphylos spp.

Manzanitas are very likely the best known members of the heath family with a number of species found throughout the temperate and colder regions of the world. Plants in this family seem to prefer acid soils. Manzanitas are handsome shrubs with reddish, artistically crooked stems. About fifty species of manzanita are found primarily along the coastal areas of North and Central America. Some of the species grow into mat-forming shrubs, while others are tree-like. The leaves are usually gray-green covered with fine hair and arranged in a vertical position along the stems. The flowers are bisexual, white or pinkish, urn-shaped and found in terminal clusters. The fruit is a berry or drupe consisting of several stony nutlets and a soft pulp. Some species are completely destroyed by fire, while others can crown-sprout after fire. Pink-bract manzanita, *A. pringlei,* has no capacity to crown-sprout after fire. This species reaches four meters in height and is usually found on slopes between 4000 and 7500 feet. Several species within this family are used ornamentally, while others are used for food and oils. Cranberries, blueberries and huckleberries are some of the smaller-flowered species.

Madrone

Heath Family
(Ericaceae)

Arbutus menziesii

Madrone is a beautiful small tree that has a limited distribution in southern California and is found as far north as British Columbia. This tree is reportedly located only below 5000 feet in a few places in the San Gabriel Mountains and in San Diego County. Madrone distinguishes itself with a scaly, red bark that looks like the manzanita bark. The leaves of this tree are elliptic, alternate and bright green. The flowers are typically urn-shaped, whitish and develop into clusters of red-orange berries. The wood is fine-grained and has been used for making tools and ornaments. Most of the large populations of these trees are found in northern California along the Oregon-California border.

California Huckleberry

Heath Family
(Ericaceae)

Vaccinium ovatum

This is the only species of huckleberry found in southern California. This stout, much-branched shrub reaches a height of only one meter here. The leaf blades are leathery, evergreen, oblong-ovate and arranged alternately on the stems. The flowers appearing in the spring are pink, bell-shaped racemes. This species occurs from sea level to 2400 feet in dry canyons and slopes. The fruit is black and edible. Several different species grow throughout the Sierras and the Rocky Mountains. Local people make annual trips to regions where these shrubs grow to pick the juicy berries for jams and jellies.

Pink-bract Manzanita
Madrone

Manzanita
California Huckleberry

California-Bay

Umbellularia californica

California-bay, sometimes called the California-laurel, is the only native laurel found in California. This tree is called Oregon-myrtle by Oregonians and has been referred to historically as pepperwood because of its aromatic qualities. Plants within this family are centered in the tropics; common members with special economic importance are avocado, cinnamon and camphor. Bay trees grow to twenty meters in canyons and valleys below 5000 feet. The leaves are evergreen, simple, oblong and arranged alternately. When crushed the leaves give off a pungent odor that can be a source of headaches. The flowers are yellowish in early spring and develop into plum-like drupes sometimes called peppernuts. The dried fruits are used to make breads and cakes, and the volatile oil has been used both as a flea repellent and as a treatment for rheumatism.

Big-leaf Maple

Acer macrophyllum

This beautiful tree is one of three species of *Acer* found on the Pacific coast. Most of the 120 species of this family occur on the east coast and in other regions of the north temperate zone. Big-leaf maple is also referred to locally as canyon maple because it is typically found in that habitat below 3000 feet. This broad tree may reach a height of about twenty-five meters. The leaves are the largest of any American maple; they are palmately-parted, deciduous and arranged opposite each other. Greenish flowers and new leaves appear together as early as March. The fruit is a samara with two wings and two seeds borne in clusters. The U.S. Department of Agriculture claims that sap production by the big-leaf maple is nearly as good as that of the eastern sugar maple. *A. macrophyllum* will survive up to 200 years. Mountain maple, *A. glabrum,* is a dwarf maple that grows up to six meters tall. The leaves are miniature maple leaves. The fruits and flowers are also similar to those of the big-leaf maple. Mountain maple, less common in southern California, is found only between 5000 and 9000 feet in the mountains. A third maple, *A. circinatum,* vine maple, is found along the coast of northern California between 1000 and 5000 feet. All three species have had some use as ornamentals.

Box Elder

Acer negundo

Box elder is a large, roundheaded tree that reaches fifteen meters in some locations. It is found along streams and canyons below 6000 feet although not in great abundance. The deep brown bark imparts a darkened appearance to the tree. The leaves are pinnately compound with the terminal leaflet being the largest with three to five lobes. The pedicellate flowers appear slightly before the new leaves. The fruit is the typical samara found within this family. Box elders have been used in cities as ornamentals and in the country as a windbreak tree. *Acer* pollen is a source of hay fever in some persons.

44

California-Bay

Big-leaf Maple

Box Elder

Bush Mallow

Malacothamnus fasciculatus

Bush mallow is one member of a cosmopolitan family that is particularly well represented in the tropics. All southern California species of this family have five-petaled flowers with numerous stamens. The leaves are round-ovate and lobed with fine hairs on the surface giving the leaves a very soft feel. The wand-like branches bear sessile clusters of pink flowers. These shrubs, which grow up to five meters, are found below 2500 feet in inland areas on dry fans and slopes. The common cotton plant, which belongs to this family, has been under cultivation for over 2000 years. Hibiscus and hollyhock are two of the well known ornamental members of this group. Okra is the fruit of a variety of hibiscus.

Jimson Weed

Datura meteloides

Jimson weed belongs to a group of mostly tropical plants with over 100 genera found worldwide. Many species are poisonous, yet important food plants such as the potato, tomato, pepper and eggplant also belong to this family. The popular petunia and the cultivated form of tobacco are found in this group as well. Jimson weed is considered a weed that is especially obvious along roadsides. The leaves are gray-green, ovate and hairy. The flowers are typically tubular, large, white and showy. *D. discolor* is a smaller species that looks just like a miniature jimson weed. Both plants have narcotic properties. Jimson weed, also known as Jamestown weed, has been cultivated as a pot herb, which may be used to produce a highly narcotic drink that has been known to be fatal.

Tree Tobacco

Nicotiana glauca

A native plant of South America, this small tree is found below 3000 feet in waste places. Tree tobacco is easily recognized in the field by its persistent, tubular, yellow flowers seen most of the year and the gray-green, ovate leaves. This tree has very rapid growth reaching three meters after one year of development. Narcotic and poisonous properties have also been attributed to it.

Nightshade

Solanum xanti

This is an extremely large genus with over 100 species found mostly in the tropics. Several of these species are poisonous. Flower color may differentiate two common species: *Solanum douglasii* has white flowers, and *S. xanti* has purple flowers. The fruits of these plants are small tomato-like berries. It is dangerous to smoke or eat any part of them. Desert thorn, *Lycium spp.,* is a common member of this family found in desert areas. These shrubs are spiny, densely branched with clusters of spade-like leaves. The berries are edible. Ten species of *Lycium* are found in the deserts of southern California.

Bush Mallow

Tree Tobacco

Jimson Weed

Nightshade

Coast Live Oak

Oak Family
(Fagaceae)

Quercus agrifolia

Coast live oak is one of the thirty species of *Quercus* the U.S. Department of Agriculture lists as important forest trees in the country. At least twelve of these species occur in southern California. Hybridization among the species makes positive identification very difficult if not impossible in some cases. Coast live oak is usually found below 3000 feet in valleys and canyons where there is adequate moisture. Sometimes called the holly-leaf oak, it matures into a broad tree up to twenty-five meters in height, and its prickly, cup-shaped leaves (reminiscent of holly) and slender acorns are useful field identification characteristics. Tiny hairs can be seen in the axils of the leaf veins on the under surface. Over-grazing has ruined the natural regeneration of this species.

Canyon Oak

Oak Family
(Fagaceae)

Quercus chrysolepis

This tree is also known by several other common names such as maul oak, golden cup oak or iron oak and is a highly variable species adapted to moist canyons and open flats below 6500 feet. The leaves persist for three to four years and possess either entire or prickly margins. The fine hair that covers their under surface creates a lightly colored appearance. The acorns require two years to mature. During the first year they are covered with a yellow, powdery fuzz. Canyon oak is one of the most valuable species economically. The wood has been used for making wagons, flooring, furniture, and as firewood. Canyon oak is more common on the desert slopes of mountains than on the coastal sides.

Scrub Oak

Oak Family
(Fagaceae)

Quercus dumosa

Scrub oak and the less common desert scrub oak, *Q. turbinella,* are found in many areas below 5000 feet. These two species probably hybridize freely making it almost impossible to tell them apart. The leaves are either entire or spiny at the margins. The tendency for the acorns to persist on the shrubs for long periods constitutes one of the field identification characteristics. *Q. dumosa* is usually found nearer to the coast, while *Q. turbinella* is usually found in warmer habitats.

Valley Oak

Oak Family
(Fagaceae)

Quercus lobata

The stately valley oak is the tree that gives Thousand Oaks, California its name. This oak is commonly found growing in areas below 2000 feet in the San Fernando Valley and in a few other areas of Los Angeles County. This tree is very tall, reaching heights up to thirty-five meters. It has a rounded, open head and an almost stately appearance. The specific name is in reference to its deeply lobed, deciduous leaves. Acorns are produced and mature in one year. Valley oaks are good indicators of deep, rich soils. The wood is of poor quality and used mainly for firewood. Valley oaks are slowly disappearing as the human population expands.

Coast Live Oak   **Canyon Oak**

Scrub Oak   **Valley Oak**

Black Oak

Oak Family
(Fagaceae)

Quercus kelloggii

This handsome tree is the largest deciduous oak that grows in the Pacific Northwest. It reaches twenty-five meters in height. The bark is initially smooth and develops dark ridges and checks as the tree ages. The broad leaves are elliptic to obovate, bright green and nearly as large as a human hand. This species is typically found between 4000 and 8000 feet in the mountainous areas from San Diego to areas of western Oregon. The acorns were long a source of food for Indians, and many birds and mammals are dependent on them. The appearance of black oaks in the mountains is sometimes used to indicate the beginning of the montane forest. They seem to mark the transition between chaparral and montane forest plant communities. This tree is listed as a tree that causes hay fever.

Oracle Oak

Oak Family
(Fagaceae)

Quercus morehus

One of the rarely seen oaks is oracle oak, a hybrid between interior live oak, *Q. wislizenii*, and black oak, *Q. kelloggii*. This evergreen tree is usually found near black oaks and interior live oaks below 5000 feet. Oracle oak is a small tree about ten meters tall with an irregular branching pattern. The leaves are shallowly lobed and spiny looking, somewhat like the leaves of black oak. This species reportedly grows from San Diego County to northern California. One of the best places to locate this uncommon tree is near Lake Fulmor in the San Jacinto Mountains.

Interior Live Oak

Oak Family
(Fagaceae)

Quercus wislizenii

Although not particularly common in this area, this oak is an evergreen tree found growing below 5000 feet in northern California and in the San Jacinto Mountains. This tree usually grows to about fifteen meters and has a rounded top and smooth bark. The leaves are oblong and look somewhat like the leaves of canyon oak except that they are all spiny and shiny above and beneath. It is often found in the forest as a shrubby tree. There have been some attempts to grow this species of oak as a park or street tree where they become handsome specimens.

Bush Chinquapin

Oak Family
(Fagaceae)

Chrysolepis sempervirens

This forest shrub is a round-topped, low, spreading plant found within the montane forest between 6000 and 11,000 feet. This common understory shrub is recognized by its bicolor leaves, gray-green above and yellowish beneath. The leaves are oblong and lance-shaped. The fruit is an unusual chestnut-like burr with four valves containing sweet kernel seeds. Giant chinquapin, *C. chrysophylla*, is a large forest tree that grows on mountain slopes of the coast ranges in northern California. *Quercus, Chrysolepis* and *Lithocarpus* are the only three genera of this family found in southern California. *Lithocarpus densiflorus*, tanbark oak, is an evergreen tree found below 4500 feet in Ventura and Santa Barbara counties.

Black Oak   Oracle Oak

Interior Live Oak   Bush Chinquapin

Arizona Ash

Olive Family
(Oleaceae)

Fraxinus velutina

Arizona ash is Arizona's largest deciduous tree. In southern California this tree is found along streams and canyons in the Mojave and Colorado Deserts below 5000 feet. The leaves are pinnately compound with five to seven leaflets. The leaves are more than twice as large as the leaves of the flowering ash, a species more common to this area. Arizona ash grows to over ten meters in ideal habitats. The slightly leathery leaves of this species give it the alternate name of leather leaf ash.

Flowering Ash

Olive Family
(Oleaceae)

Fraxinus dipetala

This small tree is the most common member of the olive family found in southern California. Most members of this family are centered in warmer regions with only three of the twenty-five genera found worldwide occurring in this area. Flowering ashes are found below 3000 feet in the foothills with a preference for coastal mountains. The leaves are pinnately compound. The flower clusters are usually perfect and white developing into a samara. In some locations this species is found growing as a shrub and in others as a small tree.

Bush Poppy

Poppy Family
(Papaveraceae)

Dendromecon rigida

Sometimes called tree poppy, this species is the only shrub member of this family occuring in southern California. The shrub is evergreen, freely branched and inconspicuous until the flowers appear in the spring. The flowers are very showy, bright yellow, solitary and elevated away from the main body of the shrub. The leaves are simple, alternate, gray-green with very short leaf stems. The fruit is a curved capsule that does not separate even upon reaching maturity. An excellent population of bush poppy is found on desert slopes of the San Gabriel Mountains below 6000 feet.

Cat-tail

Cat-tail Family
(Typhaceae)

Typha angustifolia

Cat-tail is the only member of this family occurring in southern California. Two of the three local species are *T. angustifolia,* the narrow-leaved cat-tail, and *T. latifolia,* the wide-leaved cat-tail. They are both found in fresh-water marshes throughout the Pacific Northwest as far north as Alaska. The browning of the flower spikes during maturation provides the plant's most distinctive field characteristic. The young shoots can be eaten, and the rhizome is used to make a flour. The leaves can be used to weave baskets. These species will not grow in salt-water habitats, so they can be used as an indicator of fresh-water habitats.

Arizona Ash

Bush Poppy

Flowering Ash

Cat-tail

Palo Verde
Pea Family
(Fabaceae)

Cercidium floridum

The common name of this plant means green stick in Spanish, a name which aptly describes this small tree with distinctive green branches. The plant has a broad crown and is capable of reaching ten meters in desert washes. It is usually recognized by its unusual green, woody stems and almost leafless branches during most of the year. Small, pinnately compound leaves do appear shortly after the winter rains. Bright yellow flowers begin to appear at lower elevations in March but continue to bloom into June at higher elevations. The fruit is a flattened pod containing olive and brown seeds. The seeds have been used during hard times by Indians to make a type of ground meal. The wood of palo verde will burn, but it is not a particularly good firewood.

Broad Leaf Lotus
Pea Family
(Fabaceae)

Lotus crassifolius

This delicately branched shrub is an erect perennial with oval, pinnately compound leaves of seven to seventeen leaflets. The flowers seen in spring and summer form axillary umbels that are combinations of green, yellow and red colors. The fruit is a pod. *Lotus* grows on the banks of streams and in the flats between 2000 and 8000 feet. This is one of twenty-two species of *Lotus* that occurs in southern California. It is estimated that there may be over 150 species of *Lotus* in the world, many of which occur commonly in the northern hemisphere. Various members of the pea family are important sources of food, forage, timber and ornamentals.

Deerweed
Pea Family
(Fabaceae)

Lotus scoparius

Deerweed, also called California broom, is a very common perennial in southern California. This shrub is a small, bushy plant that usually occurs below 5000 feet in chaparral and coastal sage scrub plant communities. The leaves are pinnately compound and the flowers found in clusters in the leaf axils have a standard pea flower shape. The flowers vary in color from yellow to orange to reddish as they mature and the season progresses. Interesting recent research has shown that an intricate relationship exists between these flower color changes and the insects that pollinate them. Only two seeds are found in the slender seed pods. This is one of the first shrubs to re-colonize a habitat after fire, but eventually deerweed species are choked out by larger plants that succeed it. The plant's principle values are in soil erosion control and in their ability to fix nitrogen into the soil. Nitrogen-fixing bacteria associating with the roots of these plants convert nitrogen gas into nitrates that are useable by plants in synthesizing proteins.

Palo Verde

Broad Leaf Lotus

Deerweed

Western Redbud

Pea Family
(Fabaceae)

Cercis occidentalis

Western redbud or Judas tree, as it is sometimes called, is one of the most strikingly beautiful trees found in southern California. It is regarded as a perfect ornamental tree due in large part to slender branches, rounded leaves, pinkish-red flowers and seed pods. Western redbud grows between 400 and 5000 feet in the northern part of Los Angeles County and on the eastern side of the Laguna and Cuyamaca Mountains in San Diego County. The species has a preference for habitats with long, dry summers and cool, mild winters. The tree is used extensively as an ornamental in southern California. It rarely grows over five meters tall.

Catclaw

Pea Family
(Fabaceae)

Acacia greggii

Well adapted to dry areas, this plant is a very common, spreading, spiny shrub of the desert. Although it is generally a deciduous desert shrub, it occasionally grows into a small tree. The leaves are gray-green and characteristically bipinnate. The slender branches are armed with a great many short, curved spines. These spines are shaped like cats' claws and will pierce and catch clothing easily. The pale yellow flowers of the summer give way to a twisted seed pod in the fall. This species of *Acacia* is found in most of the desert washes below 6000 feet.

Mesquite

Pea Family
(Fabaceae)

Prosopis glandulosa

This large shrub or small tree is the most common species of mesquite occurring in the Colorado and Mojave deserts below 4000 feet. Four species of mesquite are generally found here. The leaves are typically pinnately compound; the slender, spike-shaped flowers begin blooming in April. Screwbean mesquite, *P. pubescens,* has the highly distinctive coiled seed pod. Mesquite wood has been used in the southwestern United States by pioneers and Indians for firewood, fencing and in making some types of furniture. Recently interest has developed in growing these plants commercially and harvesting them for the production of ethanol and methanol. It is feasible that existing stands could be harvested for this purpose, since it is estimated there are seventy-two million acres of mesquite growing in the Southwest.

Smoke Tree

Pea Family
(Fabaceae)

Dalea spinosa

Smoke tree, also called smokethorn, is a small, silver-gray tree that grows throughout much of the desert in sandy washes below 1500 feet. In the rising and setting sun this tree has the look of a puff of smoke. All *Dalea* have violet, pea-like flowers that develop during the late spring. The nearly leafless, spiny tree could easily go unnoticed in the absence of its flowers. The seeds of the smoke tree must be scarred in the sand before they will germinate and produce a seedling. It is this fact and the high water requirement of the species that restrict it to desert washes.

Western Redbud

Mesquite

Catclaw

Smoke Tree

Sweet Acacia

Pea Family
(Fabaceae)

Acacia farnesiana

This attractive shrub or small tree is part of the chaparral plant community in San Diego County. Sweet acacia is deciduous with pinnately compound leaves and very fragrant yellow flowers. The fruit is a cylindric pod that is slightly curved and barely open at maturity. It is likely that this plant was introduced into this area from South America during the early history of the California missions. Because of its fragrance sweet acacia is widely cultivated in countries with warm climates as a source of perfume.

Spanish Broom

Pea Family
(Fabaceae)

Spartium junceum

This is an unusual looking tall shrub with wand-like, leafless branches and bright yellow flowers during the spring months. It is another introduced-member of the pea family that has become naturalized in most areas of southern California. It is especially common along roadsides in the lower foothills. The characteristic pea flowers are a brilliant yellow and very fragrant. When Spanish broom is not flowering, it is hardly noticeable among the other chaparral shrubs. The fruit is a slender pod that opens at maturity. Very few of these shrubs are seen any distance away from the roadside, a habitat they seem to prefer.

Ironwood

Pea Family
(Fabaceae)

Olneya tesota

This symmetrical, thorny, broad-crowned tree is relatively common along desert washes below 2000 feet. Palo verde trees and ironwood trees occur together and can be mistaken for each other from a distance. Ironwood trees can reach heights up to ten meters. The leaves are small and characteristically pinnately compound. Purple pea flowers and new leaves appear together in late April and May. The twisted pods produce seeds that are reported to taste like peanuts. The wood of this species is extremely hard and durable, and has been used for making hand tools and for firewood. Ironwood trees are quite susceptible to mistletoe infestation, which weakens the trees and causes swellings along the branches. Some trees are destroyed by this parasite. In most desert areas these trees are threatened with extinction because of their repeated removal for firewood and the persistent mistletoe problem.

Sweet Acacia

Spanish Broom

Ironwood

Cinquefoil

Potentilla spp.

These shrubby plants with feather-like leaves are extremely common plants in the northern hemisphere with as many as 250 species described in the literature. The generic name makes reference to its legendary medicinal powers. In southern California about twelve species occur in varying habitats from 3000 to 10,000 feet. The name cinquefoil in French means five-leaf. The plants actually have five separate heart-shaped petals and five sepals. The flower color varies from white to yellow. The leaves are always compound, either pinnate or palmate, with definite stipules. Unlike roses this shrubby species is never thorny.

Strawberry

Fragaria vesca

Wild strawberry has cinquefoil-type flowers except that they are always white. This plant is a perennial herb with runners that form roots at the nodes. The leaves and flowers are found in basal tufts. The leaves are compound consisting of three-toothed, slightly blue-green leaflets. Typically this plant grows in shaded, moist habitats between 4000 and 5500 feet. Specially developed varieties of this species are grown commercially in the coastal valleys and flatlands throughout southern California. The large family consists of over 100 genera with 3000 species described. Besides strawberries, apples, pears, cherries, peaches, apricots, plums and almonds all belong to the rose family. There are not many wildflowers within this family.

Wild Rose

Rosa californica

This easily recognized native is an erect shrub armed with stout, flattened, and recurved prickles. The compound oval-shaped leaves consist of five to seven leaflets. The flowers are usually seen as flat-topped clusters of pink petals. There are more than 100 species of *Rosa* described in the literature for the north temperate zone, so individual species are difficult to separate. The fruit is called a rose hip, which is a good source of vitamins. The California rose is often found in shaded and moist habitats below 6000 feet in several different plant communities. Game animals browse on the shrub, and California Indians are known to have used the fruits for food and the roots to treat a variety of ailments.

Cinquefoil

Strawberry

Wild Rose

Holly-leaved Cherry

Rose Family
(Rosaceae)

Prunus ilicifolia

Holly-leaved cherry is a large, attractive shrub commonly found within the chaparral plant community growing on dry slopes below 5000 feet. This shrub is often confused with holly-leaved coffeeberry, *Rhamnus ilicifolia,* which has similar leaves and general appearance. Holly-leaved cherry has simple, glossy, wavy and spinose leaves. The flowers are found in dense, white clusters during early spring. The fruit is a drupe that first appears as a red berry and then matures to a pulpy, blackish fruit. *Prunus* is the generic name for all the stone fruits within the rose family which includes cherries, plums, peaches, apricots and almonds.

Creambush

Rose Family
(Rosaceae)

Holodiscus discolor

Creambush is a large shrub or small tree that has a wide distribution usually ranging from southern California to as far north as British Columbia. The leaves are without stipules, simple, toothed and arranged alternately. Large white flower clusters appear in early summer on plants at lower elevations. As these flowers mature, the color changes from white to pink to rust-colored. The inflorescence persists until the next year as a dried flower stalk. Creambush prefers northern exposures in shaded, moist habitats. A related species, *H. boursieri,* is a smaller, more compact shrub found between 1500 and 5700 feet in the Santa Ana Mountains and is the same species found in the Sierras.

Apache-plume

Rose Family
(Rosaceae)

Fallugia paradoxa

Apache-plume is often mistaken for *Cowania,* the cliffrose, but *Fallugia* is a much smaller shrub, never growing more than one meter high. Apache-plume bears its flowers on all pedicels. The flowers are white and solitary appearing in April and lasting until June. The leaves are very small, pinnately divided into linear divisions and arranged alternately on slender stems. Apache-plume occurs on dry slopes between 4000 and 5500 feet with junipers and pinyons. It is an evergreen shrub and does have some value as a winter forage plant. Its common name is derived from the Tewa Indian practice of making brooms and arrow shafts from the stems. It also resembles the war bonnets of the Apache Indians.

Desert Apricot

Rose Family
(Rosaceae)

Prunus fremontii

Desert apricot and desert almond, *P. fasciculata,* are both common shrubs often found at the edges of deserts below 3000 feet. Desert almond leaves are much smaller and fascicled on short, stubby branches. Desert apricot leaves are broadly ovate with short petioles. The flowers of the desert apricot are white with five petals and appear earlier than desert almond, usually in February and March. The fruit is shaped like the typical apricot fruit turning yellow-orange in the summer.

Holly-leaved Cherry

Creambush

Apache-plume

Desert Apricot

Thimbleberry

Rose Family
(Rosaceae)

Rubus parviflorus

This forest understory is a small, deciduous shrub lacking thorns found in open woods and canyons below 8000 feet. This shrub is seen as far north as the Rocky Mountains. The leaves are large, angular and palmately lobed. Cup-shaped, white flowers are found from March through August. The berries are scarlet, more tart than the raspberry, and eaten raw. Raspberry and blackberry are also species of *Rubus* although they are not quite as common as thimbleberry in this area. *R. leucodermis,* raspberry, *R. ursinus,* blackberry and the thimbleberry can be found along trails, roadsides and rocky slopes in many mountainous areas of the Pacific Northwest. Many of the members of this genus have great horticultural value.

Western Chokecherry

Rose Family
(Rosaceae)

Prunus virginiana

Western chokecherry is the common chokecherry of the United States. This shrub may grow to ten meters in ideal locations but rarely is found taller than five meters in southern California. As shrubs they can form dense thickets in moist mountain habitats below 8000 feet. The creamy white flowers hang in rachemes during the late spring and early summer. This erect shrub or small tree has smooth gray-brown bark. The abundant, dark red or black berries are an important food for small animals and birds in southern California. Because the pits of these fruits have a considerable amount of cyanide, children who have eaten a large quantity of them have suffered adverse effects. Cooking the berries releases the volatile cyanide, however, thus allowing one to prepare delicious jellies and syrups from them.

Cliffrose

Rose Family
(Rosaceae)

Cowania mexicana

This native is a freely branched shrub with shredded bark that grows three meters tall in many areas of the desert. When seen in May its flowers are cream-colored and blooming in such profusion that they cover the red-brown, glandular twigs. The leaves are small and have the appearance of tiny human hands. The leaves of a close relative, antelope bush, *Purshia glandulosa,* are very similar to those of cliffrose. Antelope bush is considered to be a more important browse species, although cliffrose is also a valuable browse plant for deer and domestic animals. The two species can be distinguished by flowers, height and location. Antelope bush has smaller pale yellow flowers, grows to two meters tall and is usually confined to the pinyon-juniper areas of the desert. Indians made cloth, mats and sandals from the silky inner bark of cliffrose. The fruits of the cliffrose develop plumy tails that resemble those of its close relative, mountain-mahogany.

Thimbleberry

Western Chokecherry

Cliffrose

Toyon

Heteromeles arbutifolia

In southern California, toyon is also known as Christmas berry because of the occurrence of its berries in December. It is an evergreen, tree-like shrub that may reach a height of ten meters. These shrubs are common members of the chaparral plant community in areas below 4000 feet. Although the flowers are inconspicuous, they later develop into berry-like pomes that are either yellow or more typically red. The leaves are elliptical to oblong and sharply toothed. The colorful berries have often been eaten raw or used to make cider; however, they are currently protected by state law. Hollywood, California derives its name from the holly-like appearance of toyon's foliage and fruits.

Mountain Mahogany

Cercocarpus ledifolius

Curl-leaf mountain mahogany is a desert slope species typically found in rocky areas between 4000 and 9000 feet. It may grow to nine meters and has distinctive leaves that are lance-elliptic with inrolled margins. *C. betuloides* is probably the most common mountain mahogany existing within the chaparral plant community on steep slopes below 6000 feet. This species has smooth, gray bark and small but prominently veined leaves. The leaves resemble those of white alder but are much smaller. Flowers appear in spring, but they are without petals. The long pistil ripens into an achene with a long, twisted tail, a field characteristic often found with this shrub. The hard wood of these species burns hot and almost smokeless.

Chamise

Adenostoma fasciculatum

Well adapted to fire, chamise is considered to be the dominant species of the chaparral plant community. This evergreen shrub covers wide areas below 5000 feet on dry ridges and steep slopes. It has small, linear, fascicled leaves. Chamise can grow to three meters and burns readily because of its high resin content. It is able to crown-sprout after fire and is usually one of the first plants to reappear after a burn. Panicles of white flowers and dried flowers appear concurrently through the early summer and late spring. *A. sparsifolium* has a more limited distribution. This shrub grows to six meters and has exfoliating reddish bark and thread-like leaves. Red shanks grows primarily on the southwestern slopes of the San Jacinto Mountains.

Serviceberry

Amelanchier pallida

Serviceberry is a large shrub growing up to five meters tall from San Diego County to Montana. The leaves are simple, entire or serrate and arranged alternately. The flowers are white and in rachemes which later develop into apple-like fruits. The fruits are eaten by many animals and used by man to prepare jams and jellies. *A. alnifolia* is a species that has some ornamental value in California. Perhaps as many as twenty species of serviceberry occur in the north temperate zone. The berries look delicious but taste very bland and are pulpy.

Toyon

Mountain Mahogany

Chamise

Serviceberry

Bushrue

Rue Family
(Rutaceae)

Cneoridium dumosum

This medium-sized native shrub is one of three genera within the rue family found in southern California. More than 100 other genera are found in Australia, Africa and South America. Bushrue is a rather small shrub that has a spreading growth pattern reaching heights only up to one or two meters. The numerous small branches bear many linear leaves. The small white flowers have four petals and develop into a small drupe. The abundant berries form the basis for the common name berryrue, still another name for this species. Bushrue occurs below 2500 feet near the coast. Other important members of the family include citrus fruits.

Squaw Currant

Saxifrage Family
(Saxifragaceae)

Ribes cereum

Squaw currant is a compact, rounded shrub that grows on rocky slopes between 5000 and 11,000 feet. It can grow to two meters tall in the Sierras, Rocky Mountains and as far north as British Columbia. It is also found in the San Jacinto and San Gabriel ranges in southern California. Squaw currant leaves are small, typically palmately-lobed, glandular and deciduous. The currants are typically without spines. The flowers are pinkish-white, have few stamens and resemble flowers within the rose family. The berries are edible although reported to cause a burning sensation if too many are eaten at once. Deer browse on this shrub.

Golden Currant

Saxifrage Family
(Saxifragaceae)

Ribes aureum

Golden currant is a thicket-forming, erect, spineless shrub growing to about two meters in areas below 8000 feet. It is a widely distributed shrub occurring in the states of Washington, South Dakota and New Mexico. In southern California golden currant is found along water courses. Its many bright yellow flowers are seen in early spring. The fruits are edible orange berries that become blue-black as they mature. This shrub is especially common in the coastal sage scrub plant community in the San Gabriel Valley. A deciduous shrub, it bears three-lobed leaves that are either entire or toothed.

Sierra Currant

Saxifrage Family
(Saxifragaceae)

Ribes nevadense

This currant grows at elevations between 4500 and 7500 feet in all mountain regions of southern California and extends as far north as Oregon. This shrub reaches heights up to three meters and is slender-stemmed with an open growth pattern. The leaves are roundish, yet lobed and bluntly toothed. The flowers have stalks and are usually rose to deep red. The mature berries are blue-black. Sierra currant is often found along streams in shaded habitats. Associating with this shrub in the San Jacinto Mountains is western azalea and mock-orange. Chaparral currant, *R. malvaceum,* occurs below 2500 feet, has larger, thicker, lobed leaves but otherwise looks like sierra currant.

Bushrue

Squaw Currant

Golden Currant

Sierra Currant

Fuchsia-flowered Gooseberry

Ribes speciosum

Saxifrage Family
(Saxifragaceae)

Fushia-flowered gooseberry is the most common species of gooseberry found in shaded canyons below 1500 feet. It is an evergreen shrub that grows to about two meters tall and has shiny, three-lobed leaves, bristly branches and nodal spines. The flowers have stalks, are drooping, tubular and reddish. The fruit is distinctively spiny, probably the spiniest of all gooseberry species. It is also the most frequently cultivated gooseberry in southern California. Two other species of gooseberry, *R. amarum,* bitter gooseberry, and *R. montigenum,* mountain gooseberry, are frequently found in varied habitats in the foothills and higher mountains. The genus *Ribes* is the alternate host for white pine blister rust. This disease can be spotted on dead branches of various gooseberries and on white bark pines of northern California.

Silk-tassel Bush

Garrya spp.

Silk-tassel Family
(Garryaceae)

Silk-tassels are evergreen shrubs or small trees with leathery leaves that are simple and exhibit an opposite arrangement. This shrub grows to about three meters tall. The flowers are small and born in pendulous catkin clusters. *G. flavescens*, found in the San Gabriel Mountains, and *G. fremontii*, found in the Santa Ana Mountains, are two of southern California's most common species. Both species are found in the mountains below 5500 feet. About fifteen species occur in western North America and are known to hybridize freely. The herbage of these shrubs contains the alkaloid garryine which is used as a tonic. The bitter nature of this tonic is the source of yet another common name, quinine bush. A few species are used as ornamentals.

Burning Bush

Euonymus occidentalis

Staff-Tree Family
(Celastraceae)

Burning bush, sometimes called mock orange, is a single local representative of a family consisting mostly of tropical plants. Burning bush has a limited distribution being found only in the San Jacinto, Palomar and Cuyamaca Mountains. This small shrub grows along streams between 5000 and 6500 feet and rarely reaches over two meters tall. Its branches are slender and whitish bearing thin, ovate leaves. The five-petaled flowers are rounded, brownish-purple and seen only during late June and July. Common associates of this shrub in the San Jacinto Mountains are sierra currants, western azaleas and bracken ferns. Many other species in the family have ornamental foliage and fruit. Burning bush can be transplanted successfully during the rainy season or started from cuttings.

Fuchsia-flowered Gooseberry

Silk-tassel Bush

Burning Bush

Laurel Sumac

Rhus laurina

This familiar member of the sumac family is a large, evergreen shrub or small tree that is common on dry slopes below 3000 feet. Laurel sumac leaves are simple, lance-oblong and slightly folded along the midrib. Although flowers and fruits are inconspicuous, the dried flower stalks persist providing a good identifying field characteristic. This shrub has little tolerance for cold and occasionally is killed by frost during the winter. It is often covered with the parasitic plant dodder, *Cuscuta spp*. Laural sumac may be particularly desirable as an ornamental because it is free from insect pests. Many other trees and shrubs in this family are sources of various oils, lacquer and tannic acid.

Lemonade Berry

Rhus integrifolia

Lemonade berry is an aromatic shrub that reaches three meters tall in areas below 2600 feet. The twigs are stout, and the leaves are simple, thick, wavy, leathery and slightly serrate. The flowers are small and pinkish-white and appear as early as February, but may continue blooming until May. The fruit is a fuzzy, sticky, reddish berry that is used in making a lemon-flavored drink. Lemonade berry is more resistant to cold than laurel sumac. The round-shaped shrub has been used as an ornamental in California for many years and is considered to be one of the most dependable shrubs used in this way. It is most often found naturally on ocean bluffs and in canyons and dry places.

Sugar Bush

Rhus ovata

Rarely found as a tree, sugar bush is a stout, evergreen shrub that reaches three meters in height. The leaves, slightly folded along the midrib, are ovate, leathery and dark green. The flowers occur in dense clusters of small, pinkish flowers. The fruit is a glandular drupe that is quite sticky and reddish. Sugar bush is usually found in the foothills below 4000 feet and mostly within the chaparral plant community. In the desert foothills large specimens can often be found growing within the pinyon pine-juniper woodland. The fruit has some limited use in making a sweet drink. Sugar bush is a desirable ornamental since it survives in a variety of soil conditions, is frost-resistant and needs little watering once it is established.

Laurel Sumac

Lemonade Berry

Sugar Bush

Poison Oak

Sumac Family
(Anacardiaceae)

Toxicodendron diversilobum

Poison oak is reportedly one of the most widespread shrubs found in California. Formerly classified as *Rhus diversiloba* its new scientific name gives an indication of the toxic nature of this shrub. Most people, full-blood Indians being an exception, develop severe dermatitis when coming in contact with this shrub. A rash can develop from contact with the twigs alone without leaves, which are dropped during the winter months. The leaves are trifoliate, variously lobed and usually toothed. New leaves are reddish, then turn glossy green, only to turn reddish again in the fall. The fruit is a small, whitish berry, and the small flowers are also white. Poison oak has a preference for shaded, moist habitats in areas below 5000 feet. This plant has been used for treating warts, rattlesnake bites and weaving baskets.

Squaw Bush

Sumac Family
(Anacardiaceae)

Rhus trilobata

Squaw bush is a small deciduous shrub that rarely grows more than two meters high. This shrub looks very similar to poison oak. The leaves are trifoliate with a terminal leaflet that is three-lobed and two, almost oval, lateral leaflets. The tiny flowers are pale yellow, appearing before the new leaves in March and April. The fruit is a fleshy berry covered with a viscid secretion. The fruit is also used to prepare a sweet drink something like lemonade. The flexible twigs have been used by California Indians to make baskets and woven mats.

Castor Bean

Spurge Family
(Euphorbiaceae)

Ricinus communis

This plant is obviously a naturalized, tree-like shrub that is found in waste places and in the coastal sage scrub plant community. The spurge family members are common in the tropics. The leaves of castor bean are extremely large, palmately five-lobed and petioled. Pinkish flowers and spiny fruits are seen during most of the year. The seeds contain a very potent poison, ricin. Some species in the family secrete a milky juice, which is also poisonous. Castor bean is named for its similarity in appearance to sheep tick, *Ricinus,* a native tick of the Mediterranean. Rubber, oils, tapioca and cassava are products from members of this family.

Pepper-tree

Sumac Family
(Anacardiaceae)

Schinus molle

This lacy tree is a native of Peru that has become naturalized in southern California. It is a commonly cultivated tree that grows to fifteen meters tall with pendulous twigs and lance-linear leaflets. The leaves are odd-pinnate, resinous and arranged alternately along slender stems. The flowers are quite small, developing into a cluster of reddish drupes. Because this evergreen is fast-growing and free from insect pests, it is a popular and desirable ornamental along city streets and around buildings. It frequently becomes naturalized in canyons.

Poison Oak

Squaw Bush

Castor Bean

Pepper-tree

Mule Fat

Sunflower Family
(Asteraceae)

Baccharis glutinosa

This common native shrub is one of the 19,000 species of this family found around the world — a group of plants second only in size to the orchid family. Unlike orchid family plants, sunflower family members are rarely found in the tropics. Most family members are recognized by their dense flower heads, mostly alternate leaves and single-seeded achenes. Mule fat is often mistaken for a willow since its leaves are lance-linear, entire or slightly toothed. Like the willows, mule fat is often found along water courses in areas below 3500 feet. The flowers can be seen most of the year. Early settlers used this shrub as a browse for their livestock. Most of the 300 species of *Baccharis* occur in South America. In southern California, coyote brush, *B. pilularis,* broom baccharis, *B. sarothroides,* and emory baccharis, *B. emoryii*, are relatively common species.

Scalebroom

Sunflower Family
(Asteraceae)

Lepidospartum squamatum

Scalebroom is a small, erect, broom-like shrub with wand-shaped branches and small, hairy, scale-like leaves. The young shoots are covered with a fine hair, while older branches turn green and are without hairs. The numerous flower heads are terminal and appear as bright yellow flower clusters during fall. Later these flowers give way to fruits that look like tufts of cotton. Scalebroom is very common in gravelly and sandy areas below 5000 feet. The range of this plant includes parts of the Sierras, eastward into Nevada and Arizona, and southward into Baja California. The Greek derivative of its specific name means "scale," which refers to the scale-like leaves on slender broom-like branches.

Rabbitbrush

Sunflower Family
(Asteraceae)

Chrysothamnus spp.

This inconspicuous shrub is usually noticed only during late summer and fall when the showy flower clusters are in full bloom. This golden-flowered shrub is a close relative of *Haplopappus* but has narrower flower heads with whorls of flower bracts. As many as thirteen species of rabbitbrush are found in North America, usually in alkaline soils. In southern California most of the species are found below 7000 feet. The leaves are narrow and very small. The shrubs usually reach about one or two meters in height and are round in shape. The fruit is an achene, rounded in cross-section and slightly angled and hairy. Some of the species of this genus yield a latex used to make rubber.

Mule Fat

Scalebroom

Rabbitbrush

Pigmy-cedar

Peucephyllum schottii

Well adapted to dry areas, this shrub is also known as desert fir because of its superficial resemblance to fir trees. The shrub is an evergreen, woody plant found in many areas of the Mojave and California Deserts. The leaves are small, linear, needle-like, resinous and scattered along trunk-like stems. The solitary flower heads are helpful in identifying this perennial. The flowers are yellow rays usually seen from December through May in most areas. This shrub is quite common in the Panamint Mountains and the Muddy Mountains of Nevada. In areas below 3000 feet they can reach heights up to two or three meters. The crushed leaves smell somewhat like a conifer.

Pine Goldenbush

Haplopappus pinifolius

Pine goldenbush is one of about twenty-five species of *Haplopappus* that originated in Mexico and are now established in the southern California area. The genus includes annuals and perennials with resinous or glandular herbage. The leaves are simple, entire or lobed with solitary or clustered flower heads. Pine goldenbush is found below 5500 feet on the coastal sides of the mountains. It grows over two meters tall and has narrow leaves like a pine and bright yellow flowers. The needles give off a pine-like smell when crushed between one's fingers. A related species, *H. linearfolius*, narrowleaf goldenbush, is found within the pinyon pine-juniper woodland nearer the desert. The matchweeds, *Gutierrezia spp.*, and rabbitbrush, *Chrysothamnus spp.*, resemble goldenbushes and frequently occur in the same kinds of habitat.

Giant Coreopsis

Coreopsis gigantea

Giant coreopsis is an unusual looking stout perennial that grows to a height of three meters along coastal areas. This species is leafless most of the year although finely dissected leaves of about a foot in length are seen in spring. The fleshy, woody trunk is irregularly branched. The flower heads contain broad, bright yellow ray flowers. The California brown pelican has been known to use this plant to build its nests on Anacapa Island during the spring. Bigelow coreopsis, *C. bigelovii*, is a common annual of the deserts covering wide areas with a carpet of yellow flowers during early April in areas below 6000 feet.

Encelia

Encelia farinosa

Encelia, also called California brittlebrush or incienso, is a common gray-green, rounded desert shrub with elevated yellow flowers. It is usually seen along the roads in southern California. The yellow ray flowers are seen from April through July. The leaves turn almost white as they age. The woody stems exude a resin, which was chewed and used to treat various body pains by the California Indians. *Encelia californica* is the similar shrub with greener leaves that occurs nearer the coast. Bush encelia, *E. frutescens*, is another smaller desert species.

Pigmy-cedar

Giant Coreopsis

Pine Goldenbush

Encelia

Sycamore

Platanus racemosa

This large tree reaches heights up to twenty-five meters in low, open canyons and dry streambeds below 4000 feet. Members of this small family are found in the temperate and tropical zones of the northern hemisphere. The bark is thin and shredding with a blotched or marbled appearance that is a field characteristic often used to identify this tree. The leaves look like those of the big-leaf maple except that they are covered with fine hair and feel softer. Their large, palmately lobed leaves are arranged alternately along the stems. The flowers are reddish, spherical clusters that look like a string of decorations hanging from the tree. The decorated appearance continues throughout the year with the persistence of the bristly ball-like fruit. Sycamore is a deciduous tree that is often planted in parks for its shade qualities. A related species, *P. wrightii,* the Arizona sycamore, is that state's largest native broadleaf tree. Sycamore pollen has been identified as a source of hay fever in some individuals.

Elephant Tree

Bursera microphylla

A very rare tree in southern California, it is the only local member of this tropical or subtropical family consisting of about fifteen genera and over 400 species. The family contains mostly aromatic, deciduous trees. The Anza-Borrego Desert is the northern limit of the elephant tree's range. Although this tree is not common here, it can be found growing in desert washes and flats with cat's claw and barrel cactus. Elephant tree has a broad base with reddish-gray branches that look somewhat like an elephant's trunk. The yellow-green bark is thin, shreds like tissue paper and smells like turpentine or varnish. At the ends of the branches are found very small, pinnate, deciduous, alternately arranged leaves. The fruit is a small, dark berry. This tree has the appearance of a very primitive or prehistoric tree. In Mexico, where several other species exist, the oils of these trees are used for tanning and dyeing.

Walnut

Juglans californica

Sometimes referred to as the southern California black walnut, it is the only member of this family native to California. This tree may grow to ten meters tall in the foothill regions below 4500 feet in southern California. The bark is deeply grooved in older specimens and usually a dark gray-brown. The leaves are pinnately compound, alternate and deciduous. The fruit is drupe-like enclosed in a husk or shell. Male flowers are found in catkins and the female flowers are in clusters. *Juglans californica* is found in the Santa Monica, San Bernardino, San Gabriel and Santa Ana Mountains. The largest populations seem to be nearest the coast. Several other species of walnut are cultivated as ornamentals, and other species are grown for their edible seeds. Walnut hardwood is used in making furniture.

Sycamore

Elephant Tree

Walnut

Black Cottonwood
Willow Family
(Salicaceae)
Populus trichocarpa

This is the tallest broadleaf tree growing in the Pacific Northwest, often reaching heights up to sixty meters in ideal habitats. Most of these broad, open-crowned trees are found below 6000 feet along streams or in rich, deep soils in open valleys. Black cottonwood is more common in northern California than in southern California. The leaves are triangular with the upper surfaces darker green than the lower ones. The leaf stems (petioles) are rounded. Male and female flowers are found on separate trees. Female flowers mature into a cluster of fruits covered with long, fine hairs that look like cotton. Seeds from the fruits are distributed over great distances by the wind. The bark of this tree gets darker and furrows as the tree ages.

Fremont Cottonwood
Willow Family
(Salicaceae)
Populus fremontii

This small tree is the most common cottonwood found in southern California. It is named after John C. Fremont, who discovered it in 1844 while on an expedition. It rarely grows more than thirty meters tall and is usually found in moist habitats below 6500 feet. The leaves are yellow-green on both surfaces, round-ovate, and the leaf stems are flattened. The wood is soft and not very durable. In the past, wood of the cottonwood was used for making crates, sugar barrels and woodenware; now it is used primarily for firewood.

Quaking Aspen
Willow Family
(Salicaceae)
Populus tremuloides

The quaking aspen is often described as the most colorful tree in the Sierras and the Rocky Mountains. Unlike cottonwoods, quaking aspen has smooth white bark and round-ovate leaves that are pale beneath. The leaves tend to droop on slender branches. Wind causes the leaves to shimmer, hence the common name. This tree has one of the widest distributions of any North American tree, occurring as far north as Alaska and as far south as Mexico. In southern California its only reported location is along Fish Creek in the San Bernardino Mountains. Since these trees are intolerant of shade, they are often seen at the edges of forests. The North American beaver, *Castor canadensis*, uses them for food and dam building.

Willow
Willow Family
(Salicaceae)
Salix spp.

These common shrubs are found around the world mostly in cooler regions. About 300 species are found in various growth forms from low, prostrate shrubs to sizeable tree-like species. It is difficult to separate the species since they share so many of the same characteristics. The leaves are entire, narrow, simple and deciduous. Most willows prefer habitats along water courses in the semi-shade. The flowers are called catkins. The twigs are pliable and have been used for making baskets. Red willow, *S. laevigata* is a common southern California species with reddish branches and smooth herbage.

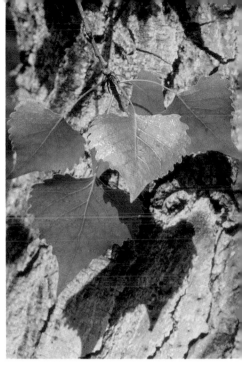

Black Cottonwood   **Fremont Cottonwood**

Quaking Aspen   **Willow**

Salt Cedar

Tamarisk Family
(Tamaricaceae)

Tamarix spp.

Although not a true cedar, this species is an introduced shrub or tree that belongs to a group of plants occurring from Mediterranean regions to the East Indies and Japan. Salt cedar is a very hardy plant that has been successfully used as a wind break along highways and railroads in the Colorado desert. These trees are becoming naturalized throughout much of the desert where the plants are usually spotted as small shrubs much greener than the surrounding vegetation. The leaves of Salt Cedar are thread-like, scaly and look like a true cedar leaf in many respects. The bark is dark reddish-brown. The flowers occur in spring as sprays of pink, catkin-like blossoms.

Poodle-dog Bush

Waterleaf Family
(Hydrophyllaceae)

Turricula parryi

Formerly *Nama parryi,* this shrub is a coarse perennial that may grow in excess of two meters tall. The herbage is glandular, ill-smelling and can cause a severe case of dermatitis in some persons. The base of the plant has a woody character. This odd-looking shrub is seen blooming from June through August. The flowers are typically tubular and lavender. The leaves are lance-shaped, slightly toothed and arranged alternately in crowded fashion along the stems. They appear somewhat like a poodle dog's fur as they die and begin to droop. The species is particularly common in the San Gabriel Mountains in areas that have recently burned.

Yerba Santa

Waterleaf Family
(Hydrophyllaceae)

Eriodictyon trichocalyx

Smooth yerba santa is a common aromatic shrub growing within several different plant communities below 8000 feet. The leaves of this species are lance-shaped, veiny and glandular with fine hairs underneath. They look as if they have been sprayed with oil. The flowers are tubular and purple. *E. crassifolium,* wooly yerba santa grows a little taller (three meters) than the former species and is usually found at slightly higher elevations. The leaves of the wooly variety have soft hairs growing on both surfaces making them appear white, shaggy and very thick. The flowers of this species are also purple and tubular.

Wax-myrtle

Wax-myrtle Family
(Myricaceae)

Myrica californica

Wax-myrtle is the only representative of this small family of trees and shrubs found in southern California. This evergreen tree or large shrub grows best in semi-moist habitats along the coast below 500 feet. It will reach heights up to five meters. The bark is smooth and gray-brown. The leaves are oblong, glossy and slightly lighter in color underneath. The small flowers begin to appear in March and April and develop into a small nut. Wax-myrtles have been cultivated in California since 1849 and used as specimen trees and hedges. The distribution of this species is limited to the Santa Monica Mountains extending north into the state of Washington.

Salt Cedar

Yerba Santa

Poodle-dog Bush

Wax-myrtle

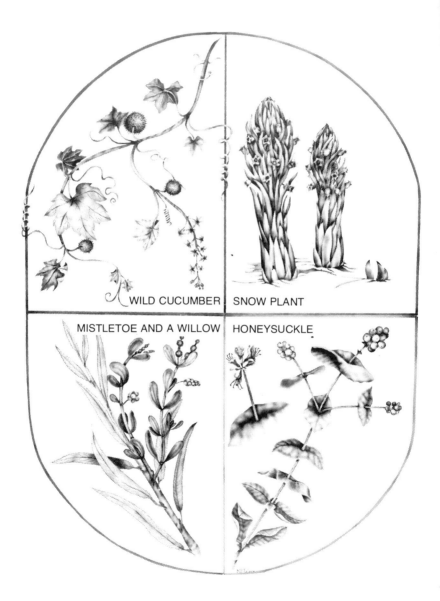

WILD CUCUMBER SNOW PLANT

MISTLETOE AND A WILLOW HONEYSUCKLE

Vines, Climbers
and Parasites

The vines and climbing plants in southern California are best represented by wild cucumber and wild grape. Both plants are excellent climbers producing tendrils for clinging to other trees and shrubs. The vines and climbers are rarely found as erect shrubs. These plants grow over, around and sometimes through shrubs and trees in several plant communities.

Plants classified as parasitic include hemiparasitic mistletoes and the completely parasitic fleshy herbs, like snow plant and pine drops. Mistletoe has chlorophyll so is capable of producing its own food photosynthetically. Mistletoe species do gain some of their nutrients from the larger host trees and shrubs, however. Since completely parasitic plants lack chlorophyll, they must obtain all their nutrients from the host plant. Snow plant and pine drops are two well known parasites that derive nourishment from fungus-root associations (mycorrhiza). These associations are complex relationships between tree roots (the host) and certain fungi, which, in turn, directly benefit the fleshy, parasitic plants.

Honeysuckle

Lonicera subspicata

The honeysuckles are a group of erect twining shrubs found chiefly in the north temperate zone. The leaves are simple, entire and arranged opposite along slender stems. The uppermost pair of leaves of several common species are joined together at the base. The flowers are seen in spring and summer as terminal spikes, axillary clusters or heads. The fruit is a few-seeded berry. Most of the five species of honeysuckle found in this area occur below 6000 feet on dry slopes or sometimes along streams. They are either erect or sprawling over the ground and other shrubs. The genus includes about 100 species worldwide.

Wild Pea

Lathyrus laetiflorus

This pea is an annual or perennial herb that has either erect or twining stems. The leaves are pinnate with the rachis modified into a tendril. The flowers are solitary or in axillary rachemes usually white or purple. Most species are found below 5000 feet within the chaparral or coastal sage scrub plant communities. The pea flowers are seen from April through June. The seed pods are usually flat, two-valved and filled with several seeds. It is not uncommon to see any one of eight southern California species growing through the top of other shrubs.

Wild Cucumber

Marah macrocarpus

Wild cucumber is a climbing herb with numerous tendrils and simple, palmately-lobed leaves. The flowers appear in axillary rachemes or panicles. The fruit is a large, spiny structure that is unlike any other fruit found in this area. The seeds are also large and brownish-gray. Wild cucumber is known for its huge, underground tuber somewhat reminiscent of a mummy in a squatting position. It is commonly called man-root because of this odd appearance. Its bitter tasting juice is poisonous. Wild cucumber is a common member of plant communities found below 3000 feet. Most of the family is tropical being cultivated widely for food. Pumpkin, squash, melons and salad cucumbers belong to the genus *Cucurbita*.

Wild Grape

Vitis girdiana

Wild grape is the only member of this primarily tropical family that grows in this area. The family consists of woody vines that climb by tendrils. The leaves are simple, palmate, petioled, deciduous and arranged alternately along twining stems. The leaves look similar to the leaves of wild cucumber. Small flowers occur in branched clusters and develop into juicy berries that are very bitter and pulpy. Wild grape is found along streams and in canyons below 4000 feet. *Vitis vinifera* is the species of grape used to make wines, grape sugar and raisins.

Honeysuckle

Wild Cucumber

Wild Pea

Wild Grape

Snow Plant

Heath Family
(Ericaceae)

Sarcodes sanquinea

One of the most unusual plants growing, the snow plant is a reddish parasitic plant found in the montane forests of the San Gabriel, San Jacinto and Santa Rosa Mountains. It is also found as far north as Oregon and in Nevada. This unusual plant grows beneath conifers in open sites between 4000 and 8000 feet. These plants are fleshy with scale-like leaves and urn-shaped flower bracts which are seen during May and June. The iridescent red color of snow plants contrasts strikingly with the green needles of its host. This non-photosynthetic plant has a fungus-root association with conifers that is mycorrhizal in nature. See the introduction of this section for a discussion of this type of relationship.

Pine Drops

Heath Family
(Ericaceae)

Pterospora andromedea

Pine drops is a small root parasite that lives primarily on fungi and the roots of conifers. This plant is more slender than the snow plant and does not appear until mid-summer. It is a dull, reddish-brown color with scale-like leaves covered with sticky hairs. The flowers are typically urn-shaped like the rest of the members of the heath family and are sometimes pink and nodding. Pine drops occur in the montane forest between 5000 and 9000 feet in most of the Pacific Northwest.

Bedstraw

Bedstraw Family
(Rubiaceae)

Galium spp.

Bedstraw is a member of a large genus of annual or perennial herbs that are often seen as shrubby plants. The presence of many subspecies makes it very difficult to separate the species. This is another family that has its center of distribution in the tropics. The plant is very delicate, often twining and often overlooked since it is small. The stems are typically four-angled. The small leaves are found in whorls along these stems, and tiny flowers are located in the axils of these leaves. Over 300 species have been described in the literature. If enough of its herbage is collected, a mattress for use outdoors can be made, a trick the early pioneers no doubt discovered.

Morning-glory

Morning-glory Family
(Convolvulaceae)

Calystegia macrostegia

Morning-glory is a climbing shrub with slender stems that wrap around any available plant or object. The triangular leaves are light green, and the stems are covered with a fine hair. The tubular, white flowers are often purple-striped when in full bloom during mid-summer. This plant may become an obnoxious weed in lawns and flower gardens in southern California. Morning-glory is very common in areas below 3000 feet. This family is centered in warmer regions where about 50 genera and 1100 species occur.

Snow Plant
Bedstraw

Pine Drops
Morning-glory

Dodder

Morning-glory Family
(Convolvulaceae)

Cuscuta spp.

Dodder is a hairy, parasitic plant without chlorophyll that occurs in many habitats below 5000 feet. This orange-yellow, slender-stemmed parasite is very conspicuous in the field as it grows over various shrubs. Dodder, also called witch's hair, seems almost to have a preference for growing on laural sumac. The leaves are reduced to minute scales. The flowers are also very small, perfect and waxy-white. About twelve of the more than 100 species are found in southern California. Morning-glory family members range from parasitic plants to obnoxious weeds and food plants like the sweet potato.

Mistletoe

Mistletoe Family
(Viscaceae)

Arceuthobium spp.

Mistletoe plants are shrubby half-parasites that are found all over the world. Almost every species of conifer has its own distinctive species of mistletoe. These parasites often cause the branches of the host to swell as the mistletoe grows into the plant. Mistletoe produces some of its own food photosynthetically, so its chance of surviving for a period apart from its host is very good. The leaves are reduced to scales, and the small flowers are found in the axils of the bracts. The seeds are spread by birds as they feed, and they can also be ejected from the fruits. These seeds may land on another host, stick to its branches and germinate there. Mistletoe in this area is commonly seen infecting oaks, mesquite, ironwood, cypresses, junipers, firs and pines. Branches are weakened by these infestations. *Phoradendron spp.* is the mistletoe that inhabits many deciduous trees in this area.

Virgin's Bower

Buttercup Family
(Ranunculaceae)

Clematis lasiantha

Virgin's bower is a woody climber that grows over trees and shrubs in open areas and canyons below 6000 feet. *Clematis* is a half-woody vine that climbs by means of twining petioles. The leaves are variable but usually found as leaflets, broadly ovate and deciduous with distinct petioles. The flowers are whitish with four or five sepals, no petals and numerous stamens. Large, fluffy seed heads give maturing fruits the appearance of a fuzzy ball during mid-summer. Of the 200 species occurring in temperate regions only three species are found in southern California. Many species have a horticultural importance. Although *C. lasiantha* has been grown ornamentally, it is not very popular because it is deciduous. Tea which is a useful treatment for a headache can be made from this plant.

Dodder

Mistletoe

Virgin's Bower

JOSHUA TREE

PRICKLY PEAR

LIVE-FOREVER

WHITE SAGE

94

Cacti, Sages
and Succulents

The plants in this section are so grouped primarily because they live in arid habitats, in salty soils, in the deserts or near the coast. Most of the species are found in the mint and cactus families although a few species from the ice plant, goosefoot, palm, ocotillo, sunflower and agave families are included.

Cacti, desert roses, and California deserts seem to go together. Surprisingly, the cacti are abundant only where there are seasonal rains and well-drained soils. Ten of the sixteen genera of cacti that occur in the United States are found in southern California, mostly in the hot deserts. The density of cacti in the Colorado Desert is greater than in the Mojave Desert.

Great basin sage (sunflower family) is the dominant shrub of colder deserts but is found in scattered locations throughout southern California. Bur sage (sunflower family) is the most common sage of the Mojave and the Colorado deserts. White sage (mint family) has a high-density growth pattern in the coastal Santa Ana Mountains. Other sages range from sea level to higher elevation habitats.

There are a great many succulents growing along coastal areas that are not native plants. Some of these plants have escaped from gardens and have become naturalized in some areas of southern California. These fleshy or juicy plants store considerable quantities of water. Many of them have been used ornamentally and in erosion control.

Another large group of plants that are mostly xerophytic are members of the agave family, i.e., the yuccas and their allies. These plants have long narrow leaves with sharp edges and points. Arid areas in southern California provide ideal habitats for three genera from this family.

Beavertail Cactus

Cactus Family
(Cactaceae)

Opuntia basilaris

This widespread native is a very distinctive form of cactus with brilliant magenta or white flowers but without spines. The bluish-green stems are low-spreading and bear spicules which are sharp enough to penetrate one's fingers. The rose-colored flowers are seen in April and May. This cactus grows up to the 6000-foot level. California Indians used the fruits and stems for food after removing the spicules.

Silver Cholla

Cactus Family
(Cactaceae)

Opuntia echinocarpa

In the literature silver cholla is described as the most common of the chollas from sea level to 6000 feet. The flowers are greenish-yellow, and the sprawling stems are covered with spines. This cactus is easily recognized by its slender stems and many short, spreading branches. The jumping cholla, *O. bigelovii,* is extremely common on desert fans and benches below 3000 feet. This cholla also has yellowish flowers and small fruits that are almost spineless. The seeds are incapable of germinating, so the usual method of propagation is by the branches falling on the ground and rooting there.

Barrel Cactus

Cactus Family
(Cactaceae)

Ferocactus acanthodes

This well-known barrel cactus is an erect, unbranched cactus usually found below 2000 feet in the eastern Mojave Desert and on the southwestern borders of the Colorado Desert to Baja. Barrel cactus is seen leaning toward the most intense light. This tendency starts when the cactus is a seedling and persists through maturity. The cactus can grow to over two meters tall. This spring-flowering species has between twenty and twenty-eight ribs and stores an alkaline juice that could be used as a source of water in an emergency. It is estimated that the barrel cactus lives up to thirty years. The southwest barrel cactus, *F. wislizenii*, is not found in southern California but only in Arizona where it blooms throughout the summer.

Hedgehog Cactus

Cactus Family
(Cactaceae)

Echinocereus engelmannii

Hedgehog cactus is one of the more common species of hedgehog that is sometimes also called calico or strawberry cactus because of its many-colored spines. The flowers, which are purple to lavender, close at night and reopen in the morning. This cactus is reported to be the most abundant species of cactus in California from sea level to 7000 feet. The fruits of some varieties are edible and constitute an important food for birds and rodents.

Beavertail Cactus

Silver Cholla

Barrel Cactus

Hedgehog Cactus

Prickly Pear   *Opuntia spp.*

Cactus Family
(Cactaceae)

The prickly pears all have a series of flat, jointed stems. The separation of *Opuntia species* is very difficult and partly arbitrary since in many places the cultivated species hybridize with the native species. Apparently fire has been a major factor in the evolution of prickly pears in southern California. Prickly pears rarely survive the fire that burns over the chaparral every 5 to 30 years. The flowers of this cactus vary from yellow to pink appearing in the early spring. The fruits, called tunas, are purple when mature. They can be eaten raw or made into a syrup.

Basin Sagebrush
Artemesia tridentata

Sunflower Family
(Asteraceae)

This sagebrush is an evergreen shrub that is named after the Great Basin Desert where it is the dominant shrub. In southern California it grows at elevations between 1500 and 10,000 feet. The basin sage grows to about three meters tall, has shredding bark, gray-green, three-toothed leaves and inconspicuous flowers. Members of this family are strongly aromatic, and the sage odor is a useful characteristic in their identification. The leaves can be used for making a tea drink. The pollen of this plant is known to cause hay fever. Coastal sagebrush, *A. californica,* is another one of the thirteen species of *Artemesia* found in southern California. This shrub is never very noticeable with its narrow, gray-green leaves and small greenish flowers. It is used as an indicator plant within the coastal sage scrub plant community in habitats below 2500 feet. The volatile substances that produce the sage odor are so strong that even insects, like fleas and bed-bugs, are said to be repelled by the leaves if a few are placed into bed rolls and sleeping bags.

Ocotillo
Fouquieria splendens

Ocotillo Family
(Fouquieriaceae)

This unusual looking plant is a resinous, spiny, spectacular desert shrub. It has green, photosynthesizing stems and small, bright green leaves that appear only during cool, wet months and fall off quickly when warm weather comes. The spines give this shrub a cactus-like appearance although they are not related to these plants. When the plant reaches about two meters tall, flame-shaped clusters of scarlet flowers appear at the ends of the branches. This shrub is extremely hardy. Those few plants destroyed naturally are uprooted by wind or floods. Some limited use of the ocotillo has occurred when desert dwellers established a hedge-row fence system. This kind of fence can be effective since the branches are extremely spiny and tough.

Prickly Pear

Basin Sagebrush

Ocotillo

Black Sage
Mint Family
(Lamiaceae)

Salvia mellifera

This aromatic shrub is very commonly found on dry slopes in southern California. Black sage is one of the members of the coastal sage scrub plant community. It grows to about two meters tall in ideal conditions. The leaves are elliptical, dark green above, slightly wooly and lighter beneath. The flowers are found in compact whorls and are usually pale blue to white. These flowers bloom from April to June. Black sage has long been considered by bee keepers to be one of the best sources of honey in this area.

Wand Sage
Mint Family
(Lamiaceae)

Salvia vaseyi

Wand sage is one of the nineteen species of *Salvia* native to California. All of the species have the characteristic mint pungency. The mint family itself is centered in the Mediterranean region with about 150 genera found throughout the world. Some plants in this family are a source of oils while others have become established as ornamentals and weeds. Other than the minty odor, another field characteristic used to help identify these plants is the presence of four-cornered stems. Wand sage is centered near the Colorado Desert below 2500 feet. The stems of this species are unusually long and wand-like with white flowers found at the ends of the branchlets.

Desert Lavender
Mint Family
(Lamiaceae)

Hyptis emoryi

This member of the mint family is a common shrub of the deserts. Most members of this genus are found in South America. Desert lavender is the only representative of this genus found in California. Apparently its distribution is limited by the periodic presence of frost as it is rarely found in areas that are not protected and at lower elevations. The herbage is typically wooly and the branches are slender with many axillary purple flowers in the spring. Desert lavender attracts bees so is sometimes called the bee sage. After rain this sage is known to smell a little like turpentine. Goats and sheep browse on this plant.

White Sage
Mint Family
(Lamiaceae)

Salvia apiana

White sage is one of the most common aromatic sages constituting one of the dominant species of the coastal sage scrub plant community. There are areas in the Santa Ana Mountains near the coast where this species completely covers the hillsides. The leaves of white sage are covered with minute hairs thus giving the herbage a very pale-green appearance. The flower stalks are very prominent and give rise in spring months to lavender-white flowers loosely grouped in bunches. White sage is reported to hybridize freely with wand sage and black sage.

Black Sage

Wand Sage

Desert Lavender

White Sage

Horehound

Mint Family
(Lamiaceae)

Marrubium vulgare

Horehound is a small introduced plant from the region around the Mediterranean Sea. In southern California it occupies waste places at lower elevations and habitats within several different plant communities. Small, white, axillary flowers occur in the spring. Later these flowers produce a spiny, burr-type fruit that clings to clothing very easily. The sap of this species is quite bitter, but when sweetened it can be used to make the well-known horehound candy.

Bladder-sage

Mint Family
(Lamiaceae)

Salazaria mexicana

Bladder-sage or paper-bag bush is a small, inconspicuous, intricately branched shrub with spiny branches. Probably the most interesting aspect of this shrub is the unusual flower with a calyx that becomes inflated into a swollen pod upon maturing. The dry sacs look something like chinese lanterns. These small shrubs are found in arid areas below 5000 feet near deserts. Desert ground squirrels will open the papery pods and extract the seeds as a source of food.

Mugwort

Sunflower Family
(Asteraceae)

Artemisia douglasiana

Mugwort is one of thirteen species of *Artemisia* found in southern California. All the sages in this family have the characteristic strong sage odor. Mugwort is found in waste places below 6000 feet. Its leaves are discolored with green tops and gray-green bottoms. Near the coast *A. californica* is the common sage with dull gray-green, thread-like leaves and shredded, woody bark. Basin sagebrush, *A. tridentata,* is found further inland in southern California and is the dominant shrub of the Great Basin Desert to the north. The leaves of these species can be used to make a tea. Pioneers are reported to have used sage leaves to drive off fleas from their bedrolls.

Desert Trumpet

Buckwheat Family
(Polygonaceae)

Eriogonum inflatum

This unique plant of the deserts has unusual inflated pipe-like stems and basal leaves. This perennial plant occurs in both southern California deserts in washes and mesas below the 6000 foot level. Old growth persists along with new growth throughout the year on this small shrub. In some areas of the Colorado Desert the inflated stems do not appear, so these plants have been separated into the variety *E. deflatum.* The flowers which bloom in the spring are quite small and yellow. The green stems can be cooked and eaten.

Horehound

Bladder-sage

Mugwort

Desert Trumpet

Joshua Tree

Agave Family
(Agavaceae)

Yucca brevifolia

Spread over wide areas of the Mojave Desert the Joshua tree sup-
posedly marks its southernmost boundary. The actual range of these
unusual trees is as far north as Utah and as far south as the Joshua
Tree National Monument in southern California. Joshua trees grow to
twelve meters tall on mesas and slopes between 2000 and 6000 feet.
The creamy-white flowers do not occur every year. They are seen only
when there is adequate rainfall and temperatures are ideal for flower
production. The leaves are bluish-green, six to ten inches long, pointed
and stiff. These bayonet-like leaves have small teeth at the edges. The
fruit is a capsule with flat black seeds that are scattered by the wind.

Mojave Yucca

Agave Family
(Agavaceae)

Yucca schidigera

Mojave yucca is also known as the Spanish dagger. This is the most
common yucca of the deserts and is easily recognized by its long,
yellow-green leaves and woody trunk. The leaves are highly fibrous
and have been used for making ropes and baskets. *Y. baccata,* Spanish
bayonet, is the rarest yucca in southern California being found only in
the eastern Mojave Desert associating with pinyon pines and junipers.
The fruits and young flower stalks of both species are supposed to be
edible.

Our Lord's Candle

Agave Family
(Agavaceae)

Yucca whipplei

Our Lord's candle is the common yucca of the chaparral and coastal
sage scrub plant communities. It is one of the four species of yucca
found in southern California with thirty-six other species occurring in
other arid locations in North America. This shrub grows in areas below
4000 feet. It is conspicuous only when it flowers and sets fruit. It dies
soon after this final flowering process. Its leaves are long, narrow,
sharp and rather stiff. This yucca is used ornamentally throughout
southern California.

Century Plant

Agave Family
(Agavaceae)

Agave deserti

Century plant or desert agave is a stemless plant with a whorl of fleshy,
sharp-tipped and sharp-edged leaves. Desert agave is distributed
throughout both the high and low deserts in washes and slopes below
5000 feet. The flower stalks bear yellow flowers in late May. Flowering
is very infrequent (purportedly once a century) and as soon as the fruit
is mature, the rest of the plant dies. The young flower stems are edible
and the fibers in the leaves have been used for making rope. In Mexico
the sap of some species of *Agave* is fermented to produce tequila.

Joshua Tree
Our Lord's Candle

Mojave Yucca
Century Plant

Parry Nolina

Agave Family
(Agavaceae)

Nolina parryi

Often mistaken for yucca, nolinas occur on rocky slopes of the San Jacinto Mountains between 3000 and 5500 feet. It is one of three species of *Nolina* native to southern California. All three species have long, narrow, grass-like leaves. This perennial looks somewhat like a yucca except that its flowers are smaller, and the male and female flowers are found on separate plants. The leaves of these species are soft enough to allow cattle and other grazing animals to eat them during times of drought.

California Fan Palm

Palm Family
(Arecaceae)

Washingtonia filifera

Suprisingly, this tree is the only native palm of southern California. Many introduced species are grown ornamentally. The leaves of the palms are five to six feet long and shaped like fans. The oval fruit is a berry or a drupe. The native palm grows to twenty-five meters tall and is found in secluded canyons and gorges in Palm Canyon. It is estimated that some of the older specimens are over 200 years old. Members of this family have enormous economic value as a source of oils, waxes, edible fruits, building materials and as ornamentals.

Live-forever

Stone-Crop Family
(Crassulaceae)

Dudleya spp.

These hardy plants represent a group of succulent herbs that are centered in South Africa. Stonecrop, *Sedum spp.*, is another common genus within this family. The separation of species within these two genera is difficult. Twenty-three species of *Dudleya,* which hybridize freely, occur in California alone. The range of these succulents is from sea level to over 9000 feet. Live-forever is usually found in shaded habitats in well-drained soils. The basal leaves are fleshy and the flowers are small varying in color from red to white and pink. These plants are extremely hardy surviving for very long periods in harsh habitats.

Ice Plant

Ice Plant Family
(Aizoaceae)

Gasoul crystallinum

Ice plant, formerly *Mesembryanthemum crystallinum,* is a true ice plant — so called because of the large vesicular cells covering the surface of the leaves and stems. The sparkling nature of these specialized cells give the appearance of crystals in the sunlight. This species is an annual with succulent leaves. The leaves turn from green to reddish as the season progresses. The flowers are small and either white or pink. Originally these plants were introduced extensively for erosion control along the coast. Now many of these plants, which are native to South Africa, Asia and Africa, have become naturalized and grow along the sea cliffs and salt marshes. Newport Back-Bay has a significant number of ice plants growing along the road.

Parry Nolina

California Fan Palm

Live-forever

Ice Plant

ottentot Fig

Ice Plant Family
(Aizoaceae)

Carpobrotus edulis

This widespread and conspicuous succulent is referred to as an ice plant but more correctly is called sea fig or Hottentot fig. Locally there are two species, a white-flowered plant and a red-flowered plant. The red-flowered plant, *C. chilense,* is a native of South America. The white-flowered plant, *C. edulis,* is a native of South Africa. Reportedly *C. edulis* is edible and was used by the Hottentots as a food plant. The leaves of both species are elongate, succulent and triangular shaped in cross section. In southern California many are used along freeways as ground cover plants and in erosion control. It has been found, however, that the heavy weight of their growth often causes slopes to slide after rains when the soil is saturated with water.

Chuparosa

Acanthus Family
(Acanthaceae)

Beloperone californica

Chuparosa is a small shrub of the desert with often leafless branches. The generic name refers to its dart-like axillary red flowers. The stems are gray-green and thickly covered with stiff hairs. The small, slender leaves drop off in the fall leaving the rounded shrub almost naked. Chuparosa is found at low elevations in sandy washes and among rocks in the Colorado Desert. The flowers are a source of nectar that attracts sparrows and hummingbirds. There are 200 genera and 2000 species within the family worldwide, although this species is the only one native to southern California. Many of the species found in warmer regions are prized ornamentals.

Saltbush

Goosefoot Family
(Chenopodiaceae)

Atriplex lentiformis

Wingscale or fourwing saltbush is a large, erect, woody shrub with gray, scaly branches. Over one hundred species of this shrub are distributed in many parts of the world. In southern California the species occurs primarily in alkaline and sandy soils in the Colorado and Mojave deserts. Wingscale has conspicuous wings arising from the fruiting bracts and seeds. Desert Indians used to grind the seeds into a meal that was used in their cooking. Other parts of the plant have been ground into a powder, mixed with water and used as a treatment for various insect bites. This species is one of the most widely distributed of the saltbushes and is valuable as a grazing shrub in the deserts.

Hottentot Fig

Chuparosa

Saltbush

White Forget-me-not

Borage Family
(Boraginaceae)

Cryptantha spp.

White forget-me-not, *Cryptantha spp.*, and popcorn flower *Plagiobothrys spp.*, are both slender, hairy plants with mostly basal leaves and small white flowers usually in a coil. Popcorn flower is found in moister habitats. *Cryptantha* has a wider distribution occurring as far inland as the desert. There are about 100 genera and 2000 species within this family distributed mostly in warmer or temperate regions. The borage family is closely related to the phacelia family and is sometimes confused with it because its flowers are strung along a coiled stalk. Several species of forget-me-nots are grown as ornamentals.

Bur-sage

Sunflower Family
(Asteraceae)

Ambrosia dumosa

Bur-sage or burro-weed is a small desert shrub almost as common as creosote bush in many areas. Upon close inspection this shrub reveals an intricate branching pattern and distinctively lobed leaves. The flowers are small and white, pollinated primarily by the wind. The fruit is a tiny bur that clings to animals and the clothing of people brushing against it. The bur-sage is tender enough for animals to use it as forage. It is rare above 5500 feet and prefers well drained soils.

Desert Tobacco

Nightshade Family
(Solanaceae)

Nicotiana trigonophylla

The small, dull green desert tobacco is a desert perennial that grows in low, rocky canyons and washes. In ideal sites this plant can reach about one to two feet high. The herbage is dark green and the distinctive tubular flowers are white. Most parts of the plant are ill-smelling. Apparently several Indian tribes smoke it. The herb is named after the Frenchman, Jean Nicot, who introduced tobacco into France.

Cheesebush

Sunflower Family
(Asteraceae)

Hymenoclea salsola

One of the most common plants of the desert, this rounded shrub is usually found in the same habitats as bur-sage and desert tobacco. In ideal habitats cheesebush grows to nearly two meters tall and from a distance looks like a tumbleweed. The unisexual flowers are very inconspicuous and small. They are surrounded by several membranous scales, a characteristic that is useful in field identification. New growth has a faint odor of cheese when it is crushed between one's fingers.

White Forget-me-not

Desert Tobacco

Bur-sage

Cheesebush

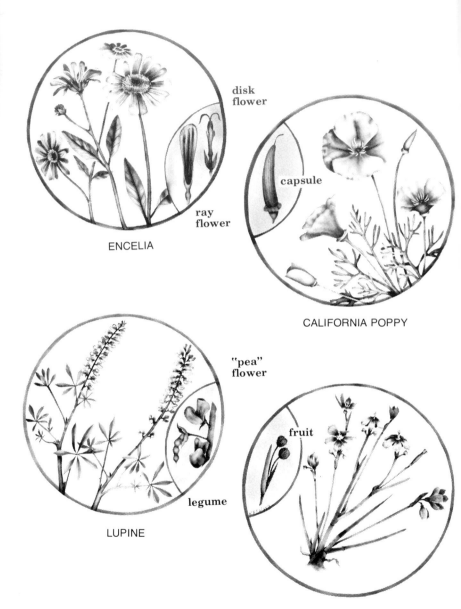

disk
flower

ray
flower

ENCELIA

capsule

CALIFORNIA POPPY

"pea"
flower

legume

LUPINE

fruit

BLUE-EYED GRASS

112

Wildflowers

The plants included in this section are often found growing in open fields or woodlands. Wildflowers, also called herbs, are non-woody plants, either annuals or perennials and native to southern California. In this area the wildflowers begin making their appearance in February and persist until the latter part of May in lower elevations.

The flower, usually showy and a delight to our senses, is the reproductive organ of angiosperms. The female part of the flower (pistil) contains the ovules which will later develop into seeds. The male part of the flower (stamens) produces the pollen that must somehow be transferred to the pistil if the ovules and seeds are to develop. The pollination process is aided by wind or by insects. Insect pollination represents a specialized, mutually beneficial process between the flower for facilitating fertilization and the insect for acquiring nectar.

Wildflowers selected for this field guide are mostly the conspicuous ones that can be seen while on a hike or driving along a road. They are organized in the standard way according to the color of their flowers. Color variations are very common, making it necessary to use other field characteristics for positive identification. The wildflowers belong to several different plant families; determining the proper family will often help in identification of the unknown plant. Some of the most obvious plant family characteristics are as follows:

1. Plants with milky juice belong to the milkweed or spurge families.
2. Plants with their flowers in umbels belong to the carrot or primrose families.
3. Plants with narrow, coiled influorescence are in the borage, phlox or waterleaf families.
4. Plants with four petals and sepals and six stamens are in the mustard family.
5. Plants with a corolla of jointed petals with distinct upper and lower lips are in the mint or figwort families.
6. Plants with square stems belong to the mint family.
7. Plants that climb by tendrils are in the cucumber or grape families.
8. Plants without any green color are in the heath family.
9. Plants that have thick-jointed stems belong to the cactus family.
10. Plants living in the water are in the waterlily or plantain families.

113

Hooker's Evening Primrose

Evening-primrose Family
(Onagraceae)

Oenothera hookeri

This herb is an unusually tall (up to one meter), erect, unbranching biennial that characteristically grows in moist habitats between 5000 and 9000 feet in southern California. The leaves are lanceolate and become progressively smaller from the base of the plant to the top of the stem. In June through September large yellow flowers make this herb relatively easy to spot from along roadsides. Of the forty-two species of *Oenothera* native to California several are used in gardens. Species are distributed from the coast to the deserts.

Butter & Eggs

Figwort Family
(Scrophulariaceae)

Linaria vulgaris

Butter and eggs is also known as toadflax, a name derived from the resemblance of the corolla to a toad and the flax-like leaves. This perennial grows to one meter tall along roadsides and on the sides of mountains. Butter and eggs is native to Europe, but in many areas of North America it has escaped cultivation and grows in large patches. The flowers are pale yellow and tipped upward in a crowded spike. In the summer these plants are commonly seen in semi-moist habitats in southern California and throughout the Pacific Northwest from sea level to about 7500 feet.

Monkey Flower

Figwort Family
(Scrophulariaceae)

Mimulus spp.

Mimulus is an extremely widespread genus in North America with seventy-seven of the one hundred and fifty species occurring in California. About half of these species are annuals and the rest are perennials. Monkey flowers frequent habitats from the coast to the high mountains in dry and moist places. The flowers are common yellows to oranges and reds. Shrub-type monkey flowers are available for planting as ornamentals. The monkey-face-appearing flowers are very well adapted for pollination by bees, having small landing platforms for these insects. One of the most common species found within the chaparral and coastal sage scrub plant communities in southern California is the sticky-leaf monkey flower, *M. longiflorus*. The herbage of this species is very sticky and the flowers are orange. During spring this species is commonly seen along roads through the foothills in southern California. The shrubby species of *Mimulus* were formerly in the genus: *Diplacus*.

Hooker's Evening Primrose
Monkey Flower

Butter & Eggs
Sticky-leaf Monkey Flower

Lemon Lily

Lily Family
(Liliaceae)

Lilium parryi

One of our most beautiful herbs is a yellow-flowered perennial herb found along streams above 4000 feet in the San Gabriel and San Jacinto Mountains. The underground bulb produces scattered or lower whorls of linear leaves and trumpet-shaped yellow flowers with three sepals. The family is a very complex one with about 250 genera and up to 6000 species in the world. Many are planted as ornamentals, such as tulips and day lilies, while others such as onion and asparagus are used as food. A few species are known to be poisonous. Both the Humboldt lily *L. humboldtii* and the panther lily *L. pardalinum* are found in moist habitats in southern California mountains although less commonly than lemon lily.

Fiddleneck

Borage Family
(Boraginaceae)

Amsinckia intermedia

The fiddlenecks, often confused with some of the phacelias, are annual herbs with bristly, erect or spreading stems. The flowers are usually naked with yellow to orange corollas. *Amsinckia intermedia* is an erect, slender weed found in disturbed places along roadsides and waste places from British Columbia to southern California. This species is covered with bristly hairs and can grow to nearly one meter in favorable habitats. The arrangement of the flowers in a coiled, fiddle-scroll spike is particularly distinctive of this genus.

Brass-buttons

Sunflower Family
(Asteraceae)

Cotula coronopifolia

As the name implies, this herb has button-like flowers. It is a naturalized plant from South Africa. This perennial is a fleshy plant with small linear leaves and bright yellow disk flowers. Brass-buttons is a common plant along salt marshes near the coast in the mud or on moist banks. The button-like shape of the flowers is a consequence of the absence of ray flowers. This is not typical of most members of the sunflower family where both ray and disk flowers are usually present in one composite flower. This species is also found on Santa Catalina, Santa Cruz and Santa Rosa islands.

Lemon Lily

Fiddleneck

Brass-buttons

Golden-Yarrow

Eriophyllum confertiflorum

This showy species is a perennial plant with a woody base and is somewhat shrubby. The long, slender stems are grayish and wooly with small hairy pinnate or bipinnate leaves. The numerous flowers have four to six yellow rays and occur in the spring in rounded clusters. Golden-yarrow grows on dry slopes in the chaparral and coastal sage scrub plant communities. Common yarrow, *Achillea millefolium*, is white-flowered and even more common than golden-yarrow. At least ten different forms of common yarrow are found along trails and roadsides throughout the Pacific Northwest.

Common Sunflower

Helianthus annuus

This impressive annual can grow up in excess of two meters in ideal conditions. In southern California the Common Sunflower is seen from sea level to about 5000 feet along roadsides and other waste places except for the Mojave Desert. The large, ripened flower heads appear from June to September. The stems bear pointed-ovate leaves that have hairs stiff enough to puncture the skin. A number of the more than fifty species found in North America have been cultivated for centuries, which has caused many species to become more widespread than their normal range.

Senecio

Senecio triangularis

Senecio or arrowleaf groundsel belongs to a large group of over 1000 species worldwide. This senecio has arrowhead-shaped leaves and yellow flower clusters that are usually flattened. Groundsel, sometimes called ragwort, is found in moist habitats in the mountains from Alaska to southern California and New Mexico. All species of *Senecio* have flower bracts in a single row. The solitary flowers are found June through September. Seventeen other species of *Senecio* occur in the southern California area.

Goldfields

Lasthenia chrysostoma

This showy native is a small, slender annual with narrow, opposite leaves and reddish stems. The solitary, yellow heads hold about ten oblong rays. Sixteen related species are found in California, and one other is found in Chile. In the early spring these plants form a yellow carpet in open areas where grass is sparse. The preferred habitats are fields near the deserts or in poor soils where there is adequate seasonal moisture. The genus gets its name from the young Greek girl who attended the lectures of Plato in a man's clothes.

Golden-Yarrow

Senecio

Common Sunflower

Goldfields

California Poppy

Eschscholzia californica

California poppy has been California's state flower since 1903. About half of the twenty-six genera within the family are found in California. Most of its members are herbs or shrubs with milky juice and conspicuous flowers. The flowers have many stamens, partly united pistils and twice as many petals as sepals. The fruit, which is a capsule, is a source of heroin and morphine. All species have bright yellow or orange flowers. The deep taproots allow these plants to persist for several seasons. California poppies are seen in the Mojave Desert in February and in the mountains in September.

Golden Ear-drops

Poppy Family
(Papaveraceae)

Dicentra chysantha

Golden ear-drops, formerly of the fumatory family (Fumariaceae), has been reclassified into the poppy family. This perennial herb grows to more than one meter tall. The plant is slender with basal leaves and unusual yellow flowers. The leaves are fern-like, pinnately compound, and bluish-green. The flowers are bilateral with two petals bent at mid-length and sticking out sideways. The fruit is a pod. Golden ear-drops can be found in waste places below 5000 feet in the southern half of California to northern Baja California. It commonly recolonizes burned areas.

Blazing Star

Stick-Leaf Family
(Loasaceae)

Mentzelia spp.

Blazing star is a spectacular member of a relatively small family consisting of only fourteen genera centered in temperate and tropical America. Plants in this family have barbed hairs on the leaves that cause the leaves to stick to fabric. *Mentzelia* is the most widespread genus found in open, gravelly areas from Mexico to southeastern British Columbia. It possesses many large, star-like, lemon-yellow flowers borne on stout, white stems. The flowers with their many stamens and symmetrical shape have a star-like appearance.

Western Wallflower

Mustard Family
(Brassicaceae)

Erysimum capitatum

Western wallflower is another showy herb of the mustard family — a large family consisting of over 200 genera and 1800 species worldwide. The family name was once cruciferae in reference to its four-flower petals spread out like a Maltese cross. In addition to the four cross-forming petals, the flowers have four sepals and six stamens (two shorter than the others). Western wallflowers are found in rocky places from the coast up to 8000 feet. Family members have a watery, acrid juice and a distinctive pod-like, upright fruit. Common garden plants like cabbage, radish, turnip, cauliflower and mustard belong to this group of plants. Various species of mustard, *Brassica*, turn the foothills a golden yellow in the early spring.

California Poppy

Golden Ear-drops

Blazing Star

Western Wallflower

Mariposa-Lily

Calochortus spp.

Mariposa-lily, also known as star-tulip and butterfly-tulip, is a beautiful bulb plant that was eaten by California Indians. Seventeen of the sixty species of *Calochortus* are found in southern California, the genus being restricted to western North America. Mariposa is the Spanish name for butterfly, which refers to the goblet-shaped flowers colored primarily white but with varying amounts of red and blue. These plants grow near the coast up to 10,500 feet in southern California. Interestingly, the flowers bloom in profusion one year and then typically are not seen for one or two years, while the plants store enough energy to flower again.

Dune Primrose

Evening Primrose Family
(Onagraceae)

Oenothera deltoides

Dune primrose, also known as the birdcage evening primrose, is a grayish plant with large, white, paper-thin flowers. The leaves are basal and deltoid-shaped. The flowers turn pale pink as they mature. In some years when moisture levels are high, the sandy desert areas appear to be covered with white tissue paper when these plants are flowering. This annual flowers in April and May in both the Mojave and Colorado deserts. When the plants die, their stems coil upward and form the "birdcage" for which the plants are named.

Matilija Poppy

Poppy Family
(Papaveraceae)

Romneya coulteri

This deliciously fragrant herb is known by many as the "Queen of the California Wildflowers." The tall stems grow from half-woody bases to about two meters. *R. coulteri* hybridizes with *R. trichocalyx*, and these hybrids are grown as ornamentals. These beautiful perennials are found in the mountains near the coast in dry canyons and washes below 4000 feet during late spring and early summer. Small, gray-green, divided leaves are found along the entire plant. Large, fragrant white flowers are the most conspicuous part of these plants. The fruit is a bristly capsule.

Star-Lily

Lily Family
(Liliaceae)

Zigadenus fremontii

Star-lily is an herb with long, basal, grass-like leaves and clusters of white flowers in a raceme or branched flower clusters. This lily is found below 3500 feet on dry, grassy slopes within the chaparral and coastal sage scrub plants communities. It grows on several of the Channel Islands, and one form is found in the Santa Ynez Mountains. Although the star-lily is not poisonous, its highly poisonous relative, death camas, *Z. venenosus*, grows throughout the western United States and may poison sheep if grazed. Early settlers and Indians have been poisoned by death camas, too, when they mistook it for an edible species, such as camas lily *Camassia*.

Mariposa-Lily

Dune Primrose

Matilija Poppy

Star-Lily

Shooting Star

Dodecatheon spp.

Shooting star originates from a word meaning "protected by the gods." Most of the fourteen species are found in North America. Two species and several subspecies are located in southern California. The perennial herbs bear basal leaves with distinctive dart-like flowers that vary in color from lavender to white. The higher elevation shooting stars are usually reddish-lavender and have flowers shaped like a rocket. Only a few species have consistently white corollas. In southern California there are shooting stars found from sea level to 11,000 feet, usually in moist habitats. There are many cultivated varieties.

Prickly Poppy

Argemone munita

In the spring, the spiny perennial prickly poppy grows along roadsides up to about 6000 feet. This leafy herbaceous plant is branched, pale and bluish-green with prickles all over its stem. The leaves are prickly and lobed. The flower is large, white and showy. The fruit is a capsule. All parts of this plant are poisonous. The generic name *Argemone* means "cataract of the eye," which is supposed to be cured by this plant. Thirty other species occur in North and South America and Hawaii. Only one other species, *A. corymbosa,* is found in the Mojave Desert in southern California.

Cow Parsnip

Heracleum sphondylium

Cow parsnip is named after Hercules, who is supposed to have used this plant medicinally. The carrot family members are considered to be economically important because of the food plants, condiments, ornamentals and poisonous members of the group. Representatives of this family have their flowers born in umbels, often flat-topped, compound umbels, as in the carrot. The fruits are dry, seed-like and variously ribbed or winged and almost always strong smelling. Carrots, celery, dill, parsnip and parsley belong to this family. The herbage of several species can be poisonous, however. Poison hemlock, *Conium maculatum* is the plant that killed Socrates. Ranger's buttons, *Sphenosciadium capitellatum*, and cow parsnip are often found growing together in moist meadows up to 9000 feet. Cow parsnip is the most widespread species of the carrot family found in North America. This plant is made into a tea (a teaspoon to a cup) and drunk for nausea, acid indigestion and heartburn.

Shooting Star

Prickly Poppy

Cow Parsnip

Wild Onion

Amaryllis Family
(Amaryllidaceae)

Allium spp.

Wild onion, formerly of the lily family, is a perennial herb with bulbs and basal, linear leaves. The herbage has the taste and smell of onions. The variously colored flowers usually ranging from pink to white are borne in terminal umbels. *Allium* is a genus with over 500 species worldwide many originating in the Old World. Several plants are grown for their economic value, such as onions, garlic, chives, shallots and leaks. Various species have been used as ornamentals. Most of the eight southern California species of wild onion are found between 2000 and 8500 feet on dry slopes during the spring.

White-stemmed Milkweed

Milkweed Family
(Asclepiadaceae)

Asclepias albicans

This straggly shrub is a perennial that in ideal habitats grows up to two meters tall. The herbs, shrubs or vines of this family usually have thick milky juice and opposite or whorled leaves. There are about 250 genera and 2000 species distributed widely but concentrated primarily in tropical regions. White-stemmed milkweed is a tall, leafless, white-stemmed plant with star-like, whitish flowers in umbels. This milkweed blooms sporadically throughout the year and produces a thin capsule with seeds that can become airborne. *A. albicans* is common in rocky places in the high and low deserts below 2500 feet. Asklepios was the Greek god of medicine and some species of this genus are said to have medicinal value.

Meadow-rue

Buttercup Family
(Ranunculaceae)

Thalictrum fendleri

This delicate, perennial herb has branched stems and highly divided thin leaves. The flowers are greenish-brown, numerous and pendulous. Meadow-rue is often found as an understory plant in forests up to 10,000 feet. Moist, shaded ground is a preferred habitat of this plant. The fruit is a small, pointed, narrow structure. The common name refers to its resemblance to the common rue *(Ruta),* a plant grown for its medicinal and aromatic qualities. Various species of meadow-rue occur as far north as British Columbia.

Stinging Nettles

Nettle Family
(Urticaceae)

Urtica holosericea

Stinging nettles is a tall perennial that grows from underground rootstocks. All four genera of this family are herbaceous, although some woody species are known in the tropics. One of the world's most beautiful fibers called ramie is produced by a member of this family. Stinging nettles are unpleasant, erect plants that can grow along streams and moist places reaching heights up to three meters. The barbed hairs on the stems create a stinging irritation that is due to formic acid released when they pierce the skin. The leaves are coarsely toothed and opposite. The flowers are small, greenish and axillary. Young shoots can be boiled and eaten.

Wild Onion

White-stemmed Milkweed

Meadow-rue

Stinging Nettles

Sweet Fennel

Carrot Family
(Apiaceae)

Foeniculum vulgare

This perennial weed is naturalized from Europe. Four species occur in the Old World with only one species found in southern California. This erect, branching herb has many striations along the stiffened stems. At the top of the two-meter tall plant are found the typical umbrella-like flower clusters that are always associated with this family. The leaves are pinnately compound, and the small flowers have a yellowish appearance. This herb is usually found in waste places. When the stems are crushed, a licorice odor is noticed.

Poison-Hemlock

Carrot Family
(Apiaceae)

Conium maculatum

Poison-hemlock is another member of the apiaceae family that is a naturalized plant from Europe. This biennial herb grows to about two meters in the second season of growth. The leaflets are divided and fern-like. The flowers are white and situated in terminal clusters. The stems are hollow, jointed and branching. This weed plant is found as far north as Canada and as far east as Florida usually below 500 feet. The roots and seeds contain dangerous alkaloids and will easily kill an adult person with one mouthful. The ancient Greeks used this plant to kill political prisoners including Socrates. Wild celery, *Apiastrum angustifolium,* a non-poisonous plant, looks similar to poison-hemlock except for its coarser stems and broader leaves. Both are found along Newport Back-Bay.

Sea-Lavender

Leadwort Family
(Plumbaginaceae)

Limonium californicum

Sea-lavender or marsh-lavender is the most common southern California representative of this small family of plants usually found in saline or calcareous places. Most of the species of sea-lavender are found in the coastal salt marsh and coastal strand plant communities. The leaves are basal, oblong and reddish which is the characteristic most often used in identification of this plant. The flowers are found in loose spikes or clusters and are usually pale violet. Sea-lavender is found along the salt marshes of southern California in open places with other halophytes.

Miner's Lettuce

Purslane Family
(Portulaceae)

Claytonia perfoliata

Miner's lettuce (formerly *Montia perfoliata*) is a succulent annual that is named after John Clayton, an 18th century American botanist. This family of plants is widely distributed over the Northern Hemisphere. Miner's lettuce is an edible plant that is easily recognized by its two kinds of leaves. The basal leaves have long leaf stems, and the upper leaves form into shallow cups around the stems. The flowers are small and vary from white to pink. In southern California this species is found in shaded, moist habitats during early spring. The shoots and leaves are used as greens by some people. Chickweed, *Stellaria media*, can usually be gathered in the same location as miner's lettuce and used in salads, also.

Sweet Fennel

Poison-Hemlock

Sea-Lavender

Miner's Lettuce

Indian Paintbrush

Figwort Family
(Scrophulariaceae)

Castilleja spp.

Easily one of the best recognized flowers in the western states, *Castilleja* is a widely distributed genus with over twenty species found in southern California alone. This genus consists of over 200 species worldwide. Most plants are erect with red or orange flower tips in association with brightly colored bracts. Some of the species are known to be at least partial parasites on the roots of other plants. For this reason the plants cannot be transplanted and are also difficult to grow from seed. Most Indian paintbrushes are found in mountain meadows, thickets and forest openings. These plants bloom all through the summer in most areas of the Pacific Northwest. *C. chromosa,* desert paintbrush, is the West's most common dry-land paintbrush. The generic name honors the Spanish botanist Domingo Castillejo.

Fireweed

Evening-primrose Family
(Onagraceae)

Epilobium angustifolium

Fireweed, also known as blooming sally, is recognized by its pink spires of flowers at the ends of tall, erect stems. The leaves are long with looped veins at the margins of the leaf. There are four petals and sepals that are usually dark pink. The fruit is a pod. Fireweed grows in dense patches along roads and into the mountains often where there has been a fire. The flowering period is from June to September. All of the twelve United States genera in this family are found in California. The family is centered in the tropics and temperate zones.

Mountain Sorrel

Buckwheat Family
(Polygonaceae)

Oxyria digyna

This alpine perennial with acid juice is a high altitude mountain perennial that grows among large boulders in the alpine zones throughout the Pacific Northwest. The leaves are basal and shaped like a kidney. The flowers are mostly red to yellow-green and found in clusters at the ends of the stems. The flowers of the mountain sorrel are wind pollinated. The herbage is succulent, edible and reportedly a rich source of vitamin C. This species is found around the world at high elevations. In southern California it grows above 9400 feet.

Alum-root

Saxifrage Family
(Saxifragaceae)

Heuchera spp.

This perennial herb, often with rhizomes, is sometimes confused with mountain sorrel, *Oxyria digyna,* since both plants grow at higher elevations and do look somewhat alike. The alum-root has basal, petioled, and palmately-lobed leaves. The flowers are white to red and rather small. These plants are found in rock crevices between 5000 and 11,000 feet. The generic name is given in honor of a German medicinal botanist. Members of this family typically have flowers that are starlike; most species live in cool, moist habitats in the north temperate and arctic zones.

Indian Paintbrush   **Fireweed**

Mountain Sorrel   **Alum-root**

Peony

Peony Family
(Paeoniaceae)

Paeonia californica

Western peony or the California peony are both common names used for this handsome perennial. The foliage consists of bright green or blue-green, fleshy, dissected leaves. The plants can be found individually or in colonies along the coastal foothills below 4000 feet. Peonies are early bloomers (Feb.-Mar.). The maroon flowers are drooping, never open up, and seem overheavy for the stem. Local specimens are not nearly as beautiful as the varieties of peonies that are raised in gardens, particularly on the east coast. As many as thirty species are found in the northern hemisphere although their origins are traced into Asia. The root, a tuber, is collected and made into tea. Small quantities of tea, made with one-half teaspoon of the chopped tuber, is believed to relieve melancholia and certain types of stress. The peonies were formerly included in the Ranunculaceae.

Owl's Clover

Figwort Family
(Scrophulariaceae)

Orthocarpus purpurascens

These tiny annuals look like clover or like a small paintbrush. The flower clusters of this erect little plant are rose and yellow or rose and white with rose-purple tips. Owl's clover occurs in California, Arizona and northern Mexico in moist habitats between 2000 and 7500 feet. In the open woods and moist meadows it often covers the area with its blossoms. The Spanish name for this plant means little broom, which is descriptive of its flower cluster. The twenty-five species of owl's clover occur from Mexico to as far north as Alaska. Members of this family are highly variable in appearance and are closely related to the mints.

Mountain Heather

Heath Family
(Ericaceae)

Phyllodoce breweri

These alpine plants grow as low, matted shrubs with evergreen, fir-like leaves. The flowers are deep and bell-shaped hanging at the ends of small flower stalks. The fruit is a five-chambered capsule that splits along the walls separating the chambers. Mountain heather grows in southern California between 9000 and 11,400 feet in moist areas of the San Bernardino Mountains. This species is easily identified by its stamens, which are longer than the corolla. Various other species are found on open, rocky slopes or in forests of the high mountains as far north as Alaska. This is the only species of heather found in southern California, however.

Peony

Owl's Clover

Mountain Heather

Elephant's Head
Figwort Family
(Scrophulariaceae)
Pedicularis spp.

Elephant's head, a perennial herb, also known as lousewort, is a small plant with fern-like leaves and a racheme of reddish or yellowish flowers. These flowers are shaped like an elephant's head complete with the trunk. Three species occur in southern California in moist meadows or in dry areas between 5000 and 10,000 feet. The shortest of the lousewort species is *P. semibarbata,* whose yellowish flowers are found almost on the ground. This dwarf lousewort is found in dry, coniferous woods. It is estimated that there are over 500 species of this perennial herb found in the north temperate zone.

Scarlet Bugler
Figwort Family
(Scrophulariaceae)
Penstemon centranthifolius

Scarlet bugler is one of several species of penstemons with scarlet corollas. The generic name is derived from the Greek root words which translated means five stamens and a thread, in reference to the slender fifth stamen. The tubular, scarlet flowers are found on long stems that have very few leaves. This penstemon is found in dry open places below 6500 feet typically where the soil has been disturbed. Out of the more than 200 species of penstemons found in North America, fifty-eight are known to occur in California. It is an American genus except for a single species found in Japan.

Whorl-leaf Penstemon
Figwort Family
(Scrophulariaceae)
Keckiella ternata

The leaves of the straggly shrub are found in whorls of three near the top of the stems and in opposite arrangement near the bottom. Often the small leaves are folded along the midrib. The stems are wandlike and either erect or climbing. There are numerous scarlet flowers in an elongate inflorescence. This shrub grows to about one meter in dry slopes and canyons below 6000 feet in the San Gabriel, San Bernardino and San Diego mountains.

Heart-leaved Penstemon
Figwort Family
(Scrophulariaceae)
Keckiella cordifolia

Heart-leaved penstemon is named after David D. Keck, an American botanist and a student of the penstemons. *Keckiella* is a genus very close to *Penstemon* but differing in the degree of shrubbiness, in having nectar and lacking hairs in the corolla. This species may be a climbing shrub often seen clinging to other shrubs. It is often missed until it blooms in the late spring. Then bright red, tubular flowers and heart-shaped leaves make the plant easy to identify. This perennial can be propagated by cuttings. Heart-leaved penstemon is found growing on dry slopes and in canyons below 5000 feet.

Elephant's Head

Whorl-leaf Penstemon

Scarlet Bugler

Heart-leaved Penstemon

Scarlet Larkspur

Buttercup Family
(Ranunculaceae)

Delphinium cardinale

This tall, perennial herb is remarkable from the standpoint of its toxicity and its striking appearance within the chaparral and coastal sage scrub plant communities. The flowers are deep red, and the leaves are divided into five narrow, twisted divisions. Nine of the twenty-one genera of buttercups in the United States are found in southern California. A few of the species are used as ornamentals, and some are drug plants. These herbaceous plants are second only to locoweeds, *Astragalus spp.*, as a livestock poison. The flowers of the several species vary from reds to whites and blues. The flower always has a distinctive projecting backward spur, which gives it the common name.

Columbine

Buttercup Family
(Ranunculaceae)

Aquilegia spp.

The flowers of columbine are nodding with five spurs. It is a widespread perennial of the north temperate zone. These bushy plants have divided leaves and handsome flowers. The blue columbine, *A. coerulea,* is Colorado's state flower. Most species prefer moist habitats within mountainous regions. Columbine comes from the Latin word meaning "dove," referring to the flower's resemblance to a cluster of five doves. The genus name, *Aquilegia,* refers to the petals which are said to resemble an eagle's talons. Larkspurs, columbines, buttercups, anemones and clematis all belong to this family of variable herbs or slightly woody vines. The fruit is an achene.

Red Bush Monkey Flower

Figwort Family
(Scrophulariaceae)

Mimulus puniceus

The Red Bush Monkey Flower is an attractive, erect shrub with either smooth or pubescent herbage. The small leaves are linear-lanceolate. Bright red monkey flowers are seen from March to July. This shrub is not reported North of the Santa Ana Mountains although fairly common in San Diego County in areas below 2500 feet on dry slopes and mesas. About 150 species of *Mimulus* occur in western North America, South America, Asia and Australia. The flower is named after the comic actor, Mimus, because of the grinning corolla.

Sand-Verbena

Four-O'Clock Family
(Nyctaginaceae)

Abronia villosa

This showy desert plant is a rose-purple, much-branched annual that seems to prefer sand dunes and flats. In early spring this plant makes a beautiful show of color in open areas near the Palm Desert and Palm Springs areas. The trailing stems are hairy. The flowers are noticeably fragrant especially during evening. There are about twenty-five species of this plant in western North America. Many species can be seen growing on sandy shoulders of highways as far south as Sonora and Baja California, Mexico.

Scarlet Larkspur   **Columbine**

Red Bush Monkey Flower   **Sand-Verbena**

Fairy Duster

Pea Family
(Fabaceae)

Calliandra eriophylla

The fairy duster or hairy-leaved callindra is a low, rounded, densely branched, spreading shrub with mimosa-like leaves and long-stamened flowers. The flowers grow in clusters and give the shrub a delicate oriental appearance. This is the only southern California species. Most members of this genus are found in the tropics of Africa, Central America and India. This plant is usually found below 1000 feet in sandy washes in the Colorado Desert, northern Mexico and Texas. During periods of drought the leaves wilt badly but recover quickly after it rains.

Desert Mallow

Mallow Family
(Malvaceae)

Sphaeralcea ambigua

Desert mallow, also known as "globemallows" or "sore-eye poppies," is a desert perennial found below 4000 feet in both deserts. These plants can become quite woody, often reaching heights up to one meter. The color of the flowers varies from pink to peach or lavender. During late spring desert mallows can readily be found growing along roadsides. About half of the twenty-seven genera within this family are found in southern California. Many species are economically important because of their fibers (cotton), food value and use as ornamentals.

Mecca Aster

Sunflower Family
(Asteraceae)

Machaeranthera cognata

Mecca aster flowers vary in color from violet to lavender, sometimes being almost white. This ornamental perennial prefers to grow among rocks or in sands and clays below 500 feet. There are usually several flower heads on a single plant. The blooms are seen as early as March and continue to bloom until May. The foliage turns brown with the summer heat. The leaves are spiny and very coarse. The Mecca Hills north of the Salton Sea is an especially good habitat for these plants.

Blue Dicks

Amaryllis Family
(Amaryllidaceae)

Dichelostemma pulchella

This unusual looking herb is seen growing in between and rising above small shrubs. Blue dicks is a perennial herb with long linear leaves arising from an underground corm. The naked flower stalks appear in early spring and grow to about one-half meter. At the end of the stalk is a large compound purple flower that is rounded like an inflated ball. Actually there are many separate flowers in a crowded umbel arrangement. This herb is commonly found growing on flats and hillsides below 5000 feet as far north as the state of Utah. The amaryllis family is known for its corms, bulbs and rhizomes, which are important horticulturally.

Fairy Duster

Desert Mallow

Mecca Aster

Blue Dicks

Canterbury-bells

Waterleaf Family
(Hydrophyllaceae)

Phacelia minor

Wild Canterbury-bells or California bells is a common member of this large genus (150 species) occurring in many areas of southern California. This is an erect herb with many fine hairs and tubular, purple flowers. It is often found growing in burned-over sites or otherwise disturbed habitats. Many of the species can be recognized by their flower structure: bell-shaped corollas with stamens projecting beyond the flower crown. Some species of *Phacelia* have leaves that are twice pinnately divided and fern-like while others, like Canterbury-bells, have basal, ovate leaves.

Lupine

Pea Family
(Fabaceae)

Lupinus spp.

Lupine is a common perennial with over eighty-two species found in California. The generic name means "wolf" and was applied to these plants because they robbed the soil of its nutrients. Actually these species add beneficial nitrogen to the soil through their root nodules, but they can also produce dangerous alkaloids contained primarily in their fruits. The leaves of lupines are palmately compound. The flowers are typically pea-shaped and range in color from white to blue and purple. In southern California several species of lupines are noticeable from the roadsides during early spring. Next to the sunflower family this is one of the largest families of plants.

Centaury

Gentian Family
(Gentianaceae)

Centaureum venustum

The Centauries are supposed to have medicinal qualities. Three species occur in southern California. These erect annuals have long stalked flowers that are mostly pink or rose with white throats. The Charming Centaury has petal lobes over half as long as the flower tube. *Centaurium venustum* is found over a wide area on dry slopes and flats below 2500 feet, although sometimes found up to 6000 feet.

Iris

Iris Family
(Iridaceae)

Iris spp.

Iris belongs to a family of plants centered in South Africa and tropical America. Only five of the seventy genera in this family are found in the United States. Members of this family grow from rhizomes, corms or bulbs. The leaves are narrow and basal. The lavender flowers are showy with three petals, sepals and stamens. More than 1500 species occur in the temperate and tropical zones. Several members are a source of perfume and dyes, and many are used ornamentally. In southern California blue-eyed grass, *Sisyrinchium bellum,* is commonly found in habitats below 3000 feet. It is the most common member of this group of plants.

Canterbury-bells

Lupine

Centaury

Iris

Cardoon

Sunflower Family
(Asteraceae)

Cynara cardunculus

The Cardoon is a naturalized, thistle-like, perennial herb that is be-coming a problem in many grazing areas along the coast in Orange County. This robust plant has giant, spiny artichoke-like purple flower heads. At least two species are grown as vegetables in areas around the Mediterranean Sea. The stout stems grow to about one meter with deeply pinnate, spiny leaves. These herbs are found growing in the rolling hills east of San Francisco Bay area also. The Milk Thistle, *Silybum marianum*, is also a naturalized thistle found in many areas of California. This thistle, easily identified by its white-lined, basal leaves, is almost totally edible when prepared properly.

Prickly Phlox

Phlox Family
(Polemoniaceae)

Leptodactylon californicum

This erect, widely branched shrub is one of the most common members of the phlox family occurring in southern California. The stems are slightly woody and covered with small, prickly leaves. Many loose clumps of pink flowers cover the outer edge of the shrub. The flowers form a narrow tube and are usually pink but vary to white, cream or lilac. This family is distinguished from other related families by the presence of a regular united corolla and superior ovary. This plant blooms along roadsides from March through June in dry places below 5000 feet. The generic name refers to the finger-like divisions of the leaves. Prickly phlox is typically a cliff-hanger.

Baby Blue-eyes

Waterleaf Family
(Hydrophyllaceae)

Nemophilia menziesii

Baby blue-eyes is a sprawling succulent with blue, light blue or white flowers. The flowers are bowl-shaped blooming singly on slender stalks. The stems are branching with long, opposite, oblong leaves bearing teeth at the edges. This plant can be seen growing in moist places below 5000 feet. The flowers have five sepals, petals and sta-mens and bloom from March through June. This species is one of the best known spring wildflowers in California and has been cultivated in this country and England for over a century. A closely related species is *N. maculata*, five spot, of central California. Its flowers exhibit white petals, each with a blue-violet spot at the base.

Cardoon

Prickly Phlox

Baby Blue-eyes

FLOWER COMPONENTS

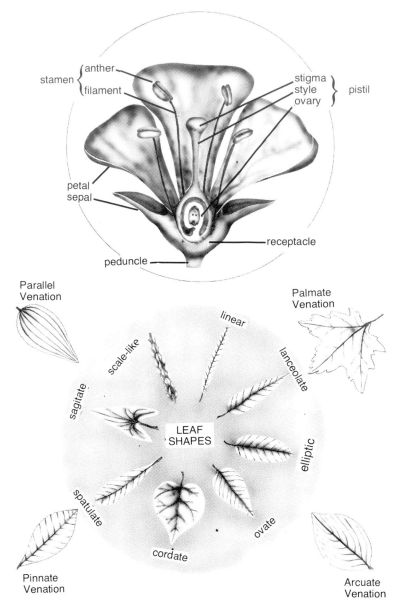

stamen {anther, filament}

stigma, style, ovary } pistil

petal
sepal

receptacle

peduncle

Parallel Venation

Palmate Venation

LEAF SHAPES

linear

scale-like

lanceolate

sagitate

elliptic

spatulate

ovate

cordate

Pinnate Venation

Arcuate Venation

Glossary

Achene. A seedlike fruit with one seed.

Alkaline. Saline or mineral salts.

Alternate Leaves. Single leaves, not in pairs.

Angiosperms. Flowering plants

Anther. Pollen portion of the stamen.

Annual. A yearly plant. Lives and dies in the same year.

Arborescent. Tree-like.

Axil. Angle created by the leaf and the stem.

Banner. Upper part of a Pea flower.

Basil Leaves. Leaves at the stem base.

Berry. Fleshy fruit, as in the tomato.

Biennial. A two year plant. Dies after two years.

Bipinnate Leaves. Compound leaves with secondary leaflets.

Bracts. Modified leaves at the flower base.

Calyx. All the sepals of the flower.

Capsule. Dry fruit, splits open at maturity.

Catkin. Scaly deciduous flower spike.

Composite Flower. Central disk flowers and surrounding ray flowers.

Compond Leaves. Leaves with divisions into leaflets.

Conifer. Cone-bearing plants.

Corm. Underground stem, like Gladiolus.

Corolla. Petals of the flower.

Deciduous. Leaves of petals falling.

Dicot. Flowering plant with flower parts in 4's or 5's, netted veined leaves.

Disk Flower. Tubular flowers in the center of composite flowers.

Drupe. Fleshy one-seeded fruit.

Endemic. Native, restricted to one area.

Exserted. Protruding, like stamens in some flowers.

Fascicled. Clusters of leaves or stems.

Fertilization. Union of the egg with the sperm.

Flora. Plants of a particular region.

Foliate. Having leaflets.

Glandular. Producing oil or nectar.

Gymnosperm. Cone-bearing plant.

Halophyte. A plant living in saline soil or salt water.

Hemiparasite. Half-parasite, like mistletoe.

Herb. Non-woody plant, usually soft.

Indicator Plants. Plants most common to one type of habitat.

Inflorescence. All flowers in a cluster.

Irregular Flowers. Petals and sepals not uniform.

Keel. Ridge or rib of a pea flower.

Lanceolate. Lance-shaped leaves, longer than wide.

Leaflet. One part of a compound leaf.

Linear. Long and extremely narrow leaves.

Lobed. Leaves with indented margins.

Monocot. Flowering plants with flower parts in 3's or multiples of 3's, leaves with parallel veins, nonwoody plants.

Montane. Coniferous forests usually over 5000 feet elevation.

Mycorrhiza. Root-fungus complexes.

Naturalized. Plants becoming part of the local flora from another region.

Native. Plants that are naturally occurring in one area.

Node. Place where leaves and stems attach.

Obovate. Inversely ovate.

Opposite. Leaves paired at a node.

Ovary. Basal portion of a pistil where seeds develop.

Ovate. Leaves that are egg-shaped.

Palmate. Leaves shaped like a human hand.

Parasite. Living organism obtaining nutrients from another live organism.

Pedicel. Stalk of a flower, also called a peduncle.

Perfect Flowers. Flowers having stamens and pistils.

Perennial. Plants living from year to year.

Perianth. Calyx and/or the corolla.

Petal. Blade of the corolla.

Petiole. Leaf stem.

Pinnate. Compound leaves with feather-like leaflets.

Pistil. Female part of a flower consisting of the stigma, style and ovary.

Pitchy. Sticky substance.

Pod. Dry fruit that opens at maturity.

Pollen. Produced by the anthers, includes the male gamete.

Pome. Apple-like fruit.

Pubescent. Covered with soft, fine hairs.

Raceme. Long inflorescence born on pedicels along a stalk.

Rachis. Axis of a spike or leaf.

Ray Flower. Flowers encircling the disk flowers.

Receptacle. Apex of the flower stalk where flower parts arise.

Regular Flowers. Petals and sepals in symmetrical arrangement, like a wheel.

Rhizome. Horizontal underground stem.

Rib. Primary vein of a leaf, ridge of cactus stem or ridge of a fruit.

Rosette. Ring of basal leaves.

Runner. Horizontal stems, like the strawberry.

Sage. Aromatic plants, either smelling like sage or mint.

Sepal. Leaf-like division of the calyx.

Serpentine. Soils that are greenish, magnesium is major component.

Serrated. Leaves with sawtooth margins.

Sessile. Leaves with no petiole or leaf stalk.

Shrub. Branching, woody plant.

Simple Leaf. Undivided leaf blade.

Sorus. Cluster of spores on fern leaf.

Spinose. Spiny, sharp-pointed.

Spore. Reproductive body of simple plants, i.e., algae, mosses, ferns.

Stamen. Male organ of a flower, the anther and filament, usually several.

Stigma. Tip of the pistil, receives the pollen.

Stipules. Leaf-like appendages on sides of some leaf stems.

Style. Narrow part of the pistil.

Succulent. Fleshy part of the water-storing leaves and stems.

Tendril. Coiled, modified leaf used in climbing.

Trifoliate. Three leaflets.

Umbel. Umbrella-like flower clusters.

Unisexual. Flowers having only stamens or pistils, only one sex.

Whorled. Leaves in a circle of three or more leaves.

Wing. Projecting membrane of a seed, leaf, leaf stalk or flower petal.

Xerophyte. Plant of an arid habitat.

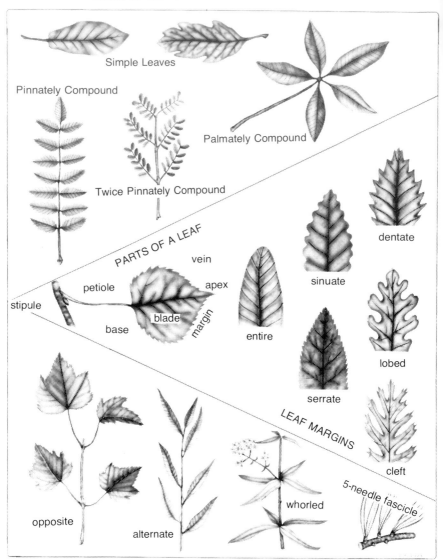

Simple Leaves

Pinnately Compound

Palmately Compound

Twice Pinnately Compound

PARTS OF A LEAF

vein

petiole

apex

stipule

base

blade

margin

entire

dentate

sinuate

lobed

serrate

cleft

LEAF MARGINS

opposite

alternate

whorled

5-needle fascicle

LEAF ARRANGEMENT

Selected References

Arno, Stephan F., 1973. *Discovering Sierra Trees*. Yosemite and Sequoia Natural History Association, U.S. Dept. of the Interior.

Balls, E. K., 1962. *Early Uses of California Plants*. California Natural History Guides, University of California Press, Berkeley.

Barbour, Michael G. and Jack Major, 1977. *Terrestrial Vegetation of California* John Wiley & Sons, New York.

Campbell, Douglas H., 1947. *Origins of California Flora*, Stanford University Press, Stanford.

Collins, Barbara J. 1972. *Key to Coastal and Chaparral Flowering Plants of Southern California* California State University Foundation, Northridge.

Coyle, Jeanette and Norman C. Roberts, 1975. *A Field Guide to the Common and Interesting Plants of Baja California* Natural History Publishing Company, LaJolla.

Critchfield W. B. and James R. Griffin, 1976. *TheDistribution of Forest Trees in California*, USDA Forest Service Research Paper, PSW - 82/1972, Berkeley.

Jaeger, Edmund C., 1969, *Desert Wildflowers*, Stanford University Press, Stanford.

Labadie, Emile L., 1978. *Native Plants for Use in the California Landscape,* Sierra City Press, Sierra City.

Lathrop, Earl W. and Robert F. Thorne, 1978. "A Flora of the Santa Ana Mountains," ALISO, 9(2), pp. 197-278.

Lenz, Lee W., 1977, *Native Plants for California Gardens*, Rancho Santa Ana Botanic Garden, Claremont

McMinn, Howard E., 1964. *An Illustrated Manual of California Shrubs*, J. W. Stacey, Inc. San Francisco.

Munz, P. A., 1974, *A Flora of Southern California*, University of California Press, Berkeley.

Munz, P. A. and David D. Keck, 1949. "California Plant Communities," ALISO, 2(1). pp. 87-105.

Niehaus, Theodore F., 1976, *A Field Guide to Pacific States' Wildflowers* Houghton Mifflin Company, Boston.

Ornduff, Robert, 1974.*Introduction to California Plant Life*, University of California Press, Berkeley.

Peattie, Donald C., 1953. *A Natural History of Western Trees*, Crown Publishers, Inc., New York.

Schmidt, Marjorie G., 1980. *Growing California Native Plants*, University of California Press, Berkeley.

Smith, Clifton F., 1976. *A Flora of the Santa Barbara Region* Santa Barbara Museum of Natural History, Santa Barbara.

Smith, James P. Jr., 1977. *Vascular Plant Families*, Mad River Press, Inc., Eureka.

Zabriskie, Jan G., 1979.*Plants of Deep Canyon*, University of California, Riverside.

Southern California Plant Families & Selected Representatives

FERNS & CONIFERS

Horsetail Family
(Equisetaceae)
Horsetail

Fern Family
(Polypodiaceae)
Bracken Fern

Ephedra Family
(Ephedraceae)
Joint fir

Cypress Family
(Cupressaceae)
Incense cedar
Cuyamaca cypress
Tecate cypress
California juniper
Utah juniper
Western juniper

Pine Family
(Pinaceae)
Coulter pine
Digger pine
Jeffrey pine
Knobcone pine
Limber pine
Lodgepole pine
Pinyon pine
Ponderosa pine
Sugar pine
Torrey pine
Big-cone Douglas fir
White fir

FLOWERING PLANTS (DICOTS)

Acanthus Family
(Acanthaceae)
Chuparosa

Barberry Family
(Berberidaceae)
Barberry

Bedstraw Family
(Rubiaceae)
Bedstraw

Bignonia Family
(Bignoniaceae)
Desert Willow

Birch Family
(Betulaceae)
Water birch
White alder

Borage Family
(Boraginaceae)
White forget-me-not

Box Family
(Buxaceae)
Jojoba

Buckeye Family
(Hippocastanaceae)
Horse-chestnut

Buckthorn Family
(Rhamnaceae)
Chaparral whitethorn
Coffeeberry
Deerbrush
Desert ceanothus
Hairy ceanothus
Holly-leaved coffeeberry

Buckwheat Family
(Polygonaceae)
Desert trumpet
Mountain sorrel
Wild buckwheat

Buttercup Family
(Ranunculaceae)
Columbine
Meadow-rue
Scarlet larkspur

Cacao Family
(Sterculiaceae)
Fremontia

Cactus Family
(Cactaceae)
Barrel cactus

Beavertail cactus
Hedgehog cactus
Silver cholla
Prickly pear cactus

Caltrop Family
(Zygophyllaceae)
Creosote bush

Caper Family
(Capparaceae)
Bladderpod

Carrot Family
(Apiaceae)
Cow parsnip
Wild celery
Poison hemlock
Sweet fennel

Dogwood Family
(Cornaceae)
Dogwood

Elm Family
(Ulmaceae)
Hackberry

Evening-primrose Family
(Onagraceae)
Dune primrose
Fireweed
Hooker's primrose

Figwort Family
(Scrophulariaceae)
Butter and Eggs
Eaton's firecracker
Elephant's head
Heart-leaved penstemon
Indian paintbrush
Owl's clover
Scarlet bugler
Scarlet monkey flower
Snapdragon penstemon

Four O'clock Family
(Nyctaginaceae)
Sand verbena

Goosefoot Family
(Chenopodiaceae)
Saltbush

Gourd Family
(Cucurbitaceae)
Wild cucumber

Grape Family
(Vitaceae)
Wild grape

Heath Family
(Ericaceae)
California huckleberry
Madrone
Mountain heather
Pine drops
Pink-bract manzanita
Snow plant
Western azalea

Honeysuckle Family
(Caprifoliaceae)
Elderberry
Honeysuckle
Snowberry

Ice Plant Family
(Aizoaceae)
Hottentot fig
Ice plant

Laurel Family
(Lauraceae)
California bay

Leadwort Family
(Plumbaginaceae)
Sea lavender

Mallow Family
(Malvaceae)
Bush mallow
Desert mallow

Maple Family
(Aceraceae)
Big leaf maple
Box elder
Mountain maple

Milkweed Family
(Asclepiadaceae)
White-stemmed milkweed

Mint Family
(Lamiaceae)
Bladder sage
Desert lavender

Horehound
Wand sage
White sage
Black sage

Mistletoe Family
(Viscaceae)
Mistletoe

Morning-glory Family
(Convolvulaceae)
Dodder
Morning glory

Mustard Family
(Brassicaceae)
Mustard
Western wallflower

Nettle Family
(Urticaceae)
Stinging nettles

Nightshade Family
(Solanaceae)
Desert thorn
Desert tobacco
Jimson weed
Nightshade
Tree tobacco

Oak Family
(Fagaceae)
Bush chinquapin
Black oak
Canyon oak
Coast live oak
Engleman oak
Interior live oak
Oracle oak
Palmer's oak
Tanbark oak
Turbinella oak
Scrub oak
Valley oak

Ocotillo Family
(Fouquieriaceae)
Ocotillo

Olive Family
(Oleaceae)
Arizona ash
Flowering ash

Pea Family
(Fabaceae)
Broad-leaf lotus
Catclaw acacia
Deerweed
Fairy duster

False indigo
Ironwood
Lupine
Mesquite
Palo verde
Smoke tree
Spanish broom
Sweet acacia
Western redbud
Wild pea

Peony Family
(Paeoniaceae)
Peony

Phlox Family
(Polemoniaceae)
Collomia
Prickly phlox

Pink Family
(Caryophyllaceae)
Chickweed

Poppy Family
(Papaveraceae)
Bush poppy
California poppy
Golden ear-drops
Matilija poppy
Prickly poppy

Primrose Family
(Primulaceae)
Shooting star

Purslane Family
(Portulacaceae)
Miner's lettuce

Rose Family
(Rosaceae)
Antelope bush
Apache-plume
Cliffrose
Cinquefoil
Creambush
Desert almond
Desert apricot
Holly-leaved cherry
Mountain mahogany
Raspberry
Red shanks
Serviceberry
Strawberry
Thimbleberry
Toyon
Western chokecherry
Wild rose

Rue Family
(Rutaceae)
Bushrue

Saxifrage Family
(Saxifragaceae)
Alum root
Chaparral currant
Fuchsia-flowered gooseberry
Golden currant
Mountain gooseberry
Sierra currant
Squaw currant

Silk-tassel Family
(Garryaceae)
Silk-tassel bush

Spurge Family
(Euphorbiaceae)
Castor bean

Staff-tree Family
(Celasteraceae)
Burning bush

Stick-leaf Family
(Loasaceae)
Blazing star

Stone-crop Family
(Crassulaceae)
Live-forever

Sumac Family
(Anacardiaceae)
Laurel sumac
Lemonade berry
Pepper tree
Poison oak
Squaw bush
Sugar bush

Sunflower Family
(Asteraceae)
Baccharis
Basin sagebrush
Brass buttons
Bur-sage
Canyon sunflower
Cheesebush
Coreopsis
Encelia
Goldenbush
Golden Yarrow
Goldfields
Mecca aster
Mugwort
Pigmy cedar
Rabbitbrush
Scalebroom
Senecio
Thistle

Sycamore Family
(Platanaceae)
Western sycamore

Tamarisk Family
(Tamaricaceae)
Salt cedar

Torchwood Family
(Burseraceae)
Elephant tree

Walnut Family
(Juglandaceae)
Walnut

Waterleaf Family
(Hydrophyllaceae)
Baby blue eyes
Phacelia
Poodle-dog bush
Yerba santa

Wax-myrtle Family
(Myricaceae)
Wax-myrtle

Willow Family
(Salicaceae)
Black cottonwood
Fremont cottonwood
Quaking aspen
Willow

FLOWERING PLANTS (MONOCOTS)
Agave Family
(Agavaceae)
Century plant
Joshua tree
Mojave yucca
Our Lord's candle
Parry nolina

Amaryllis Family
(Amaryllidaceae)
Blue dicks
Wild onion

Cat-tail Family
(Typhaceae)
Cat-tail

Iris Family
(Iridaceae)
Iris

Lily Family
(Liliaceae)
Lemon Lily
Mariposa Lily
Star lily

Palm Family
(Arecaceae)
California fan palm

Index of Common Names

Index of Scientific Names

156

METRIC SYSTEM TABLE

  1 mm. = approx. 1/25 of an inch
10 mm. = 1 cm. (approx. 2/5 of an inch)
10 cm. =   1 dm. (approx. 4 inches)
10 dm. = 1 m. (approx. 40 inches)

158

FIELD NOTES:

FIELD NOTES:

2/12/04

DATE DUE

Demco, Inc. 38-293